ISBN 978-0-331-48276-8
PIBN 11192884

N. Y.

Vassar College.

1892-93.

by-law

10 I
traveli
tising,
school
freque
circuit
expens
visits,

11 C
of teac
time a
that of
a subj

12 T
asked
and ot
justify
easier
one in

13
necessa
willing
the fol
ers, $1
uniforr
to be c

14 I
sion st
educat
reports
world,

15 S
printec
of the
swered
to his

16 T
ient pc

price, though less may be charged if financial support w
special reductions may be made to clubs, wage-earners,

TWENTY-EIGHTH

ANNUAL CATALOGUE

OF THE

OFFICERS AND STUDENTS

OF

VASSAR COLLEGE

POUGHKEEPSIE N. Y.

1892-93

POUGHKEEPSIE
A. V. HAIGHT PRINTER
1892

"It occurred to me that woman, having received from her Creator the same intellectual constitution as man, has the same right as man to intellectual culture and development."

"It is my hope to be the instrument in the hand of Providence of founding an institution which shall accomplish for young women what our colleges are accomplishing for young men."

MATTHEW VASSAR.

The College was incorporated as Vassar Female College in 1861. This name was changed in 1867 to the present corporate name, VASSAR COLLEGE.

CONTENTS.

STANDING COMMITTEES OF THE BOARD.

EXECUTIVE COMMITTEE.
J. M. TAYLOR, Chairman (*ex officio*).

D. D. PARMLY,	A. W. EVARTS,
F. F. THOMPSON,	S. D. COYKENDALL,
R. E. TAYLOR,	EDWARD ELSWORTH.

ON FACULTY AND STUDIES.
J. M. TAYLOR, Chairman (*ex officio*).

EDWARD LATHROP,	A. H. STRONG,
H. M. KING,	JOACHIM ELMENDORF,
E. G. ROBINSON,	EDWARD ELSWORTH.

ON LIBRARY.
J. M. TAYLOR, Chairman.

FLORENCE M. CUSHING,	EDWARD JUDSON,
S. D. COYKENDALL,	COLGATE HOYT,
PROFESSOR COOLEY,	PROFESSOR DRENNAN.

ON CABINETS AND APPARATUS.
A. S. BICKMORE, Chairman.

A. L. ALLEN,	JOACHIM ELMENDORF,
A. W. EVARTS,	HELEN H. BACKUS,
J. M. BRUCE,	PROFESSOR DWIGHT.

ON ART GALLERY AND ART DEPARTMENT.
CYRUS SWAN, Chairman.

D. D. PARMLY,	HELEN H. BACKUS,
GEORGE INNIS,	PROFESSOR VAN INGEN,
J. H. DEANE,	S. D. COYKENDALL.

ON MUSIC DEPARTMENT.
JOACHIM ELMENDORF, Chairman.

FREDERICK TOWNSEND,	D. D. PARMLY,
ELIZABETH E. POPPLETON,	COLGATE HOYT,
FLORENCE M. CUSHING,	L. P. MORTON.

ON SCHOLARSHIPS.
ELIZABETH E. POPPLETON, Chairman.

W. L. DEAN,	J. D. ROCKEFELLER,
N. E. WOOD,	A. J. FOX,
R. E. TAYLOR,	J. M. BRUCE.

ON FINANCE, FOR EXAMINING SECURITIES.

F. F. THOMPSON,	S. D. COYKENDALL,	D. D. PARMLY.

ON TREASURER'S ACCOUNTS.

F. F. THOMPSON,	D. D. PARMLY,	S. D. COYKENDALL.

OFFICERS OF GOVERNMENT AND INSTRUCTION.

Arranged, with the exception of the President, in each division, in order of their appointment.

———

JAMES M. TAYLOR, D.D.,

PRESIDENT,

PROFESSOR OF MENTAL AND MORAL PHILOSOPHY.

LE ROY C. COOLEY, Ph.D., (Union)

MATTHEW VASSAR, JR. PROFESSOR OF PHYSICS AND CHEMISTRY.

WILLIAM B. DWIGHT, A.M.,

JOHN GUY VASSAR PROFESSOR OF NATURAL HISTORY, AND CURATOR OF THE MUSEUM.

GEOLOGY AND MINERALOGY.

MANUEL J. DRENNAN, A.M.,

PROFESSOR OF RHETORIC, AND OF THE ENGLISH LANGUAGE AND LITERATURE.

ABBY LEACH, A.M..

PROFESSOR OF THE GREEK LANGUAGE.

LUCY MAYNARD SALMON, A.M.,

PROFESSOR OF HISTORY.

ACHSAH M. ELY, A.B.,

PROFESSOR OF MATHEMATICS.

MARY W. WHITNEY, A.M.,

PROFESSOR OF ASTRONOMY, AND DIRECTOR OF THE OBSERVATORY.

MARCELLA I. O'GRADY, S.B.,

ASSOCIATE PROFESSOR OF BIOLOGY.

HERBERT ELMER MILLS, A.M., Ph.D., (Cornell)

ASSOCIATE PROFESSOR OF HISTORY AND ECONOMICS.

JEAN C. BRACQ, A.B.,

JOHN GUY VASSAR PROFESSOR OF MODERN LANGUAGES.

FRENCH.

JOHN LEVERETT MOORE, Ph.D., (Johns Hopkins)

ASSOCIATE PROFESSOR OF THE GREEK AND LATIN LANGUAGES AND LITERATURE,

MATTHEW VASSAR, JR., FOUNDATION.

LATIN.

FRANCES A. WOOD,

LIBRARIAN.

MRS. J. RYLAND KENDRICK,

LADY PRINCIPAL.

HENRY VAN INGEN,

PROFESSOR OF ART.

EDWARD MORRIS BOWMAN, A.C.O., F.C.M.,

PROFESSOR OF MUSIC.

OTTILIE HERHOLZ,

ASSOCIATE PROFESSOR OF GERMAN.

CHARLES W. MOULTON, Ph.D., (Johns Hopkins)

ASSOCIATE PROFESSOR OF CHEMISTRY.

ELIZABETH B. THELBERG, M.D.,

PROFESSOR OF PHYSIOLOGY AND HYGIENE, AND RESIDENT PHYSICIAN.

LYDIA ANNIE WHITNEY,

TEACHER OF PIANO-FORTE PLAYING.

JESSIE CHAPIN,

TEACHER OF PIANO-FORTE PLAYING.

ELLA McCALEB, A.B.,

SECRETARY TO THE PRESIDENT.

SOPHIA F. RICHARDSON, A.B.,

TEACHER OF MATHEMATICS.

ELLA M. FREEMAN, A.B.,

TEACHER OF CHEMISTRY.

LAURA ADELLA BLISS, A.M., Mus.B.,

TEACHER OF PIANO-FORTE PLAYING AND HARMONY.

MABEL R. LOOMIS, A.B.,

TEACHER OF ENGLISH.

JENNETTE BARBOUR PERRY, A.B.,

TEACHER OF ENGLISH.

ELLA CATHERINE GREENE, A.B.,

TEACHER OF LATIN AND GREEK.

SOPHIE C. NEEF,

TEACHER OF GERMAN.

HARRIET ISABELLE BALLINTINE,

DIRECTOR OF THE GYMNASIUM.

ESTHER F. BYRNES, A.B.,

ASSISTANT IN THE BIOLOGICAL LABORATORY.

MARGUERITE SWEET, Ph.D., (Bryn Mawr)

TEACHER OF ENGLISH.

HELEN· FRANCES EPLER,

TEACHER OF FRENCH.

ADELAIDE UNDERHILL, A.B.,

ASSISTANT LIBRARIAN.

HARRIET B. ELLS,

ASSISTANT IN THE GYMNASIUM.

ALICE A. BERRY, A.B.,

TEACHER OF LATIN.

AVIS BLEWETT,

ORGANIST, AND TEACHER OF HARMONY.

ANTOINETTE CORNWELL, A.B.,

ASSISTANT IN THE OFFICES OF THE PRESIDENT AND LADY PRINCIPAL.

ELIZABETH C. PALMER, A.B.,

ASSISTANT IN THE BIOLOGICAL LABORATORY.

——— ———

TEACHER OF ELOCUTION.

JAMES ·SAUVAGE,

TEACHER OF SINGING.

CHARLES GRUBE,

TEACHER OF VIOLIN PLAYING.

PREACHERS TO THE COLLEGE.

From February, 1892, to February, 1893.

The Rev. HENRY BAKER, D.D.,	*Philadelphia.*
The Rev. WILLIAM HAYES WARD, D.D.,	*New York.*
The Rev. ALFRED H. MOMENT, D.D.,	*Boston.*
The Rev. A. J. LYMAN, D.D.,	*Brooklyn.*
The Rev. E. WINCHESTER DONALD, D.D.,	*New York.*
The Rev. H. C. MABIE,	*Boston.*
The Rev. SAMUEL H. VIRGIN, D.D.,	*New York.*
The Rev. J. B. THOMAS, D.D.,	*Newton Centre, Mass.*
The Rev. HENRY ANSTICE, D.D.,	*Rochester.*
The Rev. A. F. SHERRILL, D.D.,	*Atlanta.*
The Rev. H. L. WAYLAND, D.D.,	*Philadelphia.*
The Rt. Rev. T. F. SPALDING, D.D.,	*Denver.*
The Rev. MARVIN R. VINCENT, D.D.,	*New York.*
The Rev. L. T. TOWNSEND, D.D.,	*Boston.*
The Rev. H. P. DeFOREST, D.D.,	*Detroit.*
The Rev. B. O. TRUE, D.D.,	*Rochester.*
The Rev. EDWARD P. HART,	*Rochester.*
The Rev. A. V. RAYMOND, D.D.,	*Albany.*
The Rev. C. R. HEMPHILL, D.D.,	*Louisville.*
The Rev. HENRY M. SANDERS, D.D.,	*New York.*
The Rev. WILLIAM M. SMITH, D.D.,	*New York.*
The Rt. Rev. H. C. POTTER, D.D., L.L.D.,	*New York.*
The Rev. JAMES M. KING, D.D.,	*New York.*

NON-RESIDENT LECTURERS.

For the current year, as far as appointed, including those for 1891-'92 not mentioned in the catalogue for that year.

Miss MARY L. AVERY,	*New York.*
Professor NICHOLAS MURRAY BUTLER, Ph.D.,	
	Columbia College.
Mr. H. E. KREHBIEL,	*New York.*
Mr. PERCY M. REESE,	*Baltimore.*

PROFESSOR WOODROW WILSON, PH.D., LL.D.,
PRINCETON COLLEGE.
MR. JAMES LANE ALLEN, *Cincinnati.*
PROFESSOR BENJAMIN O. TRUE, D.D.,
ROCHESTER THEOLOGICAL SEMINARY.
THE REV. SAMUEL W. DIKE, LL.D., *Auburndale, Mass.*
MR. GEORGE L. FOX. *New Haven.*
MISS ALICE FLETCHER, *Washington.*
PROFESSOR HERBERT TUTTLE, L.H.D., CORNELL UNIVERSITY.
PROFESSOR JAMES B. GREENOUGH, HARVARD UNIVERSITY.
PROFESSOR F. W. TAUSSIG, LL.B., PH.D., HARVARD UNIVERSITY.
PROFESSOR BARRETT WENDELL, HARVARD UNIVERSITY.

STUDENTS.

GRADUATE STUDENTS.

ELLA WELBON CRAMER (Vassar, 1892), Art.
HANNAH FANCHER MACE (Vassar, 1890), Fellow in Mathematics.
SARA SHERWOOD PLATT (Vassar, 1892), Art.

SENIOR CLASS.

ADAMS, ELIZABETH KEMPER,	Nashotah, Wis.
BELCHER, FRANCES SPAULDING,	Farmington, Me.
BLAIR, MARY ELLEN,	Angelica.
BLAKE, MARION STANLEY,	Englewood, N. J.
BONNELL, CORNELIA LEAVENWORTH,	Waverly.
BRADLEY, ELIZABETH SOPHIA,	New Haven, Conn.
BROWN, ALICE CRAWFORD,	Fort Meade, S. Dak.
BROWN, MARIANNA CATHERINE,	New York.
CLARK, LILLIE BERSHA,	Hightstown, N. J.
CLARK, MARY VIDA,	Springfield, Mass.
COBB, ELIZA POLHEMUS,	Tarrytown.
CONANT, HARRIET CORINNE,	Owosso, Mich.
COOLEY, MARY ELIZABETH,	Poughkeepsie.
COOLEY, ROSSA BELLE,	Poughkeepsie.
CUTTING, ELIZABETH BROWN,	Brooklyn.
DOOLITTLE, MAY AUGUSTA,	Rochester.
EDDY, RUTH ELIZABETH.	Terre Haute, Ind.
EVANS, ETHEL RHODA,	Brooklyn.
FOSTER, FLORENCE JOSEPHINE,	Walpole, N. H.
FULLER, LOUISE ADELAIDE,	Sherburne.
GRANT, HELEN THERESE,	Detroit, Mich.
HARKER, KATHARINE VAN DYKE,	San Francisco, Cal.
HENDERSON, LIZZIE GRACE,	Pulaski.
HOLBROOK, EMMA LAURA,	Springfield, Mass.
JOLLIFFE, FRANCES BORGIA,	San Francisco, Cal.
KING, GRACE BOWEN,	Columbus, O.
KIRCHNER, WILHELMINA,	Poughkeepsie.

McDaniel, Edith,	Columbus, O.
Martin, Leonora Laval,	Memphis, Tenn.
Mathes, Mildred Overton,	Memphis, Tenn.
Morgan, Isabel Avery,	Poughkeepsie.
Neil, Edith,	Columbus, O.
O'Connell, Delia Maria,	Marlboro, Mass.
Palmer, Grace Emeline,	Washington, D. C.
Palmer, Jean Culvert,	Brooklyn.
Palmer, Ruth Ellen,	San Francisco, Cal.
Parker, Edith Maud,	La Porte, Ind.
Pratt, Henrietta Annie Rossini,	Saxtons River, Vt.
Presbrey, Blanche Dean,	Providence, R. I.
Sands, Adelaide Green,	Port Chester.
Sands, Georgiana,	Port Chester.
Schneider, Marie Sophie,	Covington, Ky.
Smith, Laura Fitch,	Moravia.
Stephens, Julia Ward,	Syracuse.
Streeter, Flora Wealthy,	Johnstown.
Van Etten, Eleanor Bristol,	Port Jervis.
Van Syckel, Anne,	Flemington, N. J.
Van Vliet, Helena,	Poughkeepsie.
Whitcomb, Adele,	Chicago, Ill.
White, Clarissa Elizabeth,	New Haven, Conn.
Wilkinson, Ethel,	Chicago, Ill.
Williams, Martha Anne,	Edgar, Ill.
Wood, Harriet Anne,	Saginaw, Mich.

JUNIOR CLASS.

Abbott, Mary Winchester,	West Haven, Conn.
Agne, Nella Landt,	Tipton, Iowa.
Andrews, Elizabeth Morehead,	Yonkers.
Barnes, Elizabeth Bowden,	Milford, Mass.
Bartlett, Emeline Barstow,	Providence, R. I.
Bernd, Florence,	Macon, Ga.
Bishoprick, Celinda Davis,	Brooklyn.
Bowman, Ina,	Philadelphia, Penn.
Boynton, Mary Louise,	Sewaren, N. J.
Brown, Irene Fowler,	Memphis, Tenn.
Carter, Edna,	Oshkosh, Wis.
Chase, Florence Adams,	Chicago, Ill.

CHATER, ELLEN DUNDAS,	Englewood, N. J.
COMAN, CAROLINE,	Hamilton.
COOLEY, GRACE WEBSTER,	Plainfield, N. J.
CRAMPTON, SUSAN CHARLOTTE,	St. Albans, Vt.
CREA, MARY LILLIAN,	Decatur, Ill.
DELANEY, JOSEPHINE,	Dallas, Texas.
ELSWORTH, ETHEL HINTON,	Poughkeepsie.
ENOS, KATE LOUISE,	Grand Rapids, Mich.
FERRELL, MARY ESTELLE,	Columbus, O.
FERRY, BLANCHE,	Detroit, Mich.
FISHER, LIZZIE GRACE,	Knowlesville.
FITCH, LUCY ALDRICH,	Skaneateles.
FITCH, MARY CLIFT,	Skaneateles.
FOWLER, CHARLOTTE LOUISA,	Poughkeepsie.
FULLER, FRANCES HOWARD, '	New York.
GEDNEY, MARY ELEANOR,	Poughkeepsie.
GILLMER, ELIZABETH ACHSA,	Warren, O.
GNADE, AGNES,	Rutherford, N. J.
GOLAY, JULIETTE,	Brewer, Me.
HAIGHT, BESSIE HAZELTON,	Auburn.
HASTINGS, MABEL LOUISE,	Brooklyn.
HEMANS, IDA MAY,	Auburn.
HENCH, LILLIE COYLE,	Harrisburg, Penn.
HILL, CLARA MOSSMAN,	Norwalk, Conn.
HOLBROOK, MYRA COFFIN,	Poughkeepsie.
HOWE, LEONORA,	Cambridge, Mass.
HUSSEY, ALICE SARAH,	Rochester.
LATIMER, ADA LOMBARD,	Memphis, Tenn.
LYNCH, MARY C.,	Chicago, Ill.
McADAMS, BESSIE MARGARET,	Mt. Pléasant, Penn.
MACARTHUR, FLORENCE BLANCHE,	Chicago, Ill.
MACAULEY, ANNIE RACHEL,	Louisville, Ky.
MACAULEY, MARY MARGARET,	Louisville, Ky.
McCARTHY, SARAH,	Rochester.
MARCHANT, MARIE,	Milwaukee, Wis.
MARSHALL, ELIZABETH ARTHUR,	Pittsburgh, Penn.
MAY, LOUISA SURRÉ,	Rochelle, Ill.
MILLER, LOUISA,	Florence, S. C.
MUMFORD, MARY BLANCHE,	Detroit, Mich.
MYERS, ANGIE MARTIN,	New York.
PATTEN, LIZZIE HIGGINS,	Newton Centre, Mass.

PATTERSON, LILA HENRY,	Franklin, Ky.
PLATT, EMILY BARTLETT,	Poughkeepsie.
ROBBINS, FLORENCE LILLIAN,	St. Paul, Minn.
SLADE, HELEN MILDRED,	Quincy, Mass.
SPIERS, KATHARINE ESTELLE,	San Francisco, Cal.
STEBBINS, KATE VAN COTT,	Rochester.
STICKNEY, RUTH,	St. Paul, Minn.
STORY, ADA BELLE,	Ouray, Col.
TODD, FLORA EDA,	Unadilla.
UTTER, KATHARINE MINERVA,	Providence, R. I.
VAILLANT, ABBY AUGUSTA,	New York.
VANDER BURGH, CAROLINE GERTRUDE,	Fall River, Mass.
VAN KLEECK, MELVINA,	Poughkeepsie.
WAGAR, HATTIE MAY,	Lakewood, O.
WELLS, EMILIE LOUISE,	St. Ignace, Mich.
WHITE, GERTRUDE,	New York.
WHYTE, LAURA AGNES,	Jersey City Heights, N. J.
WILCOX, ALICE WILSON,	Providence, R. I.

SOPHOMORE CLASS.

ABBOT, ETHELDRED,	Norwich, Conn.
ABBOTT, HARRIET ELIZABETH,	Waterbury, Conn.
ACKER, MARGARET KATE,	Poughkeepsie.
ARMSTRONG, MARY LOUISE,	Penn Yan.
ARNOLD, KATHARINE INNIS,	Poughkeepsie.
AUSTIN, SUSIE LILLIAN,	Jefferson, Mass.
BEARD, GRACE ALDEN,	Westville, Conn.
BENNETT, BEATRICE ETHEL,	Groton, Mass.
BLODGETT, CARRIE ELLIS,	West Brookfield, Mass.
BOYD, BESSIE ELIZA,	Glens Falls.
BOYNTON, GEORGIA SMITH,	Sewaren, N. J.
BRENDLINGER, MARGARET ROBINSON,	Yonkers.
BRINCKERHOFF, ANNIE MAY,	Mount Vernon.
BRONSON, GERTRUDE ANGELINE,	Cleveland, O.
BROWNELL, LAURA ANTOINETTE,	Brooklyn.
BURNHAM, PEARL VERE,	Groton, S. Dak.
CANDEE, HELEN HOLBROOK,	Poughkeepsie.
CARPENTER, GRACE,	Poughkeepsie.
CHILDS, MAY HALL,	New York.
CLARK, ADDIE LAURA,	Red Oak, Iowa.
COHEN, FANNY,	New York.

COOKE, CAROL HALL,	Poughkeepsie.
CRAWFORD, ANNIE LAZIERE,	Louisville, Ky.
DELANY, EMMA THERESA,	Chicago, Ill.
DORRANCE, ANNE,	Dorrancetown, Penn.
DOUGHTY, PHEBE VAN VLACK,	Matteawan.
DURANT, BESSIE ANNA,	Bethel, Conn.
ESTES, JENNIE AGNES,	Brooklyn.
FENTON, CAROLINE LYDIA,	Detroit, Mich.
FITCH, MARY GOODRICH,	Yonkers.
FLETCHER, JOSEPHINE BOWEN,	St. Albans, Vt.
FLETCHER, HASSELTINE REYNOLDS,	Boston. Mass.
FREEMAN, FLORENCE EDNA,	West Millbury, Mass.
GARVIN, EDITH MAY,	West Winsted, Conn.
GOODWIN, GRACE,	Thomaston, Conn.
GRAHAM, ANNA JEANETTE,	Cleveland, O.
GREER, JULIETTE,	Chicago, Ill.
GRUENING. ROSE BERTHA,	New York.
HAUGHWOUT, MARY,	Fall River, Mass.
HENRY, ALICE,	Butler, Mo.
HIGGINS, EDITH SECOR,	Stelton, N. J.
HIGMAN, ANNA CLARISSA,	Sioux City, Iowa.
HILLIER, EDDAH,	Denver, Col.
HOAGLAND, SUE WHITCOMB,	Brooklyn.
HOLMES, EDITH CLARK,	Auburn.
HOLMES, HARRIET FAY,	Oscoda, Mich.
HOLMES, HELEN MAY,	Oscoda, Mich.
HORR, ELIZABETH REED,	Dubuque, Iowa.
HOWELL, SARAH EDNA,	Port Jervis.
HULST, GRACE DURYEE,	Brooklyn.
JOHNSON, ALIDA LEWIS,	Penn Yan.
JOHNSON, WILLIE CROCKETT,	Memphis, Tenn.
JONES, MABEL IRENE,	Titusville, Penn.
KELLY, SUSAN LOUISE,	Providence, R. I.
KIRCHER, OTIE,	Davenport, Iowa.
LADUE, HELEN NEWBERRY,	Detroit, Mich.
LEARNED, ABBIE FOX,	Chicago, Ill.
McCAULEY, EMMA CORNELIA,	Stanley.
McCUTCHEON, HATTIE LOUISE,	Poughkeepsie.
McDONALD, ALICE RAMSEY,	Chicago, Ill.
McVEY, MARIA LOUISE,	Binghamton.
MARTIN, CAROLYN GRAYDON,	New York.

MERRITT, ETHEL ADAMS,	New York.
MILLARD, MARTHA MAY,	Poughkeepsie.
MONSCH, ANNA ADELE,	Louisville, Ky.
MORGAN, BERTHA DELL,	Waverly.
MUNDY, MAY SWEENEY,	Watertown.
MURRAY, EMMA WYCKOFF,	New Brunswick, N. J.
MYERS, ELSIE,	Cheyenne, Wy.
NAIRN, ALICE MARY,	Buffalo.
ORVIS, JULIA SWIFT,	Dixon, Ill.
ORWIG, MAUD,	Lansford, Penn.
PACKER, ELIZABETH ELLA.	Newton Centre, Ma .
PELGRAM, CAROLINE MARIE,	Paterson, N. J.
PICKERSGILL, LILY VIRGINIA,	Allegheny, Penn.
PIERCE, LUCY FRANCES,	Chicago, Ill.
POPPENHEIM, CHRISTIE,	Charleston, S. C.
POPPENHEIM, IDA,	Charleston, S. C.
REED, MARY MINERVA,	Sharon, Conn.
REILEY, KATHARINE CAMPBELL,	Lewiston, Penn.
REIMER, ISABELLE ADAMS,	East Orange, N. J.
RUGGE, ALICE EMMA,	Glens Falls.
SCOFIELD, JULIA AUGUSTA,	Penn Yan.
SEARING, LOUISE,	Tompkins' Cove.
SEBRING, JULIET MAY,	Kalamazoo, Mich.
SIMMONS, FLORA AMORETTE,	Worcester, Mass.
SMITH, EFFIE CLAYTON,	New Haven, Conn.
SMITH, ELIZABETH CHARD,	Watertown.
SMITH, ELIZABETH LINCOLN,	Newton Centre, Mass.
SMITH, ELEANOR LOUISE,	Dayton, O.
SMITH, FRANCES ALBEE,	Brooklyn.
SNOW, ELLA GERTRUDE,	Greenfield, Mass.
SNYDER, GABRIELLE MATILDA,	Cleveland, O.
STAMFORD, HELEN,	Grand View-on-Hudson.
STRANG, BERTHA RICH,	Yonkers.
TAYLOR, FLORA MABEL,	New York.
THORNE, ELIZABETH GERTRUDE,	Skaneateles.
TOWNSEND, WIE DURFEE,	Hudson.
TURNER, JULIA EMILY,	Quincy, Ill.
TWITCHELL, ANNA MARY,	New Haven, Conn.
UPDEGRAFF, BESS,	McGregor, Iowa.
VERHOEFF, MARY.	Louisville, Ky.
VERNON, FLORENCE IANTHE,	Brooklyn.
WATTON, MAUDE CARO,	Detroit, Mich.

WEAVER, LILLIAN CLARK,   Webster City, Iowa.
WELCH, ELLA MARIAN,   New Haven, Conn.
WHITE, GRACE ROGERS,   New York.
WILLIAMS, EDITH,   Watertown.
WITSCHIEF, GERTRUDE,   Port Jervis.
WOOD, VINNIE CLIFTON,   Fall River, Mass.
YORK, FANNY THURSTON,   Wellsville.

FRESHMAN CLASS.

ANDERSON, BELLE BINGLEY,   Melbourne, Ky.
ARNOLD, HANNAH WINIFRED,   Fall River, Mass.
BALLANCE, FLORENCE,   Peoria, Ill.
BANKS, HARRIET SKETCHLEY,   Englewood, N. J.
BARNES, CLARA ADELIA WRIGHT,   East Boston, Mass.
BARNET, BERTHA,   Chicago, Ill.
BAYLISS, LILLIAN,   Cleveland, O.
BEACH, LAURA JENNIE,   Goshen, Conn.
BELL, JESSIE,   Indianapolis, Ind.
BERLIN, LILLIAN SOUTHARD,   Wilmington. Del.
BISHOP, HELEN LOUISE,   Detroit, Mich.
BOOKER, LOUISE,   Louisville, Ky.
BRANCH, LAURA MARGUERITE,   Corning.
BRAND, NETTIE HARDIN,   Saginaw, Mich.
BROAD, MARGARET,   Buffalo.
BROWN, ANNIE ELIZABETH,   Brooklyn.
BROWN, CARRIE ETHEL,   Comstock's Bridge, Conn.
BROWN, MARGARET CAMPBELL,   Philadelphia, Penn.
CARBUTT, FLORENCE,   Philadelphia, Penn.
CHAMBERLAIN, SUSANNA WILLEY,   Chattanooga, Tenn.
CHAMPNEY, MARIA MITCHELL,   New York.
CHANDLER, SARAH FARQUHAR,   Chicago, Ill.
CHESLEY, GERTRUDE LYDIA,   Malone.
CHESLEY, MABEL LOUISA,   Malone.
CHILDS, ANNIE SMITH,   St. Albans, Vt.
CHOATE, AUGUSTA,   Atlanta, Ga.
COLLINS, LILLIAN FRANK,   Syracuse.
COOKE, JESSIE ADELIA,   Waukegan, Ill.
COONLEY, SARAH OLIPHANT,   Chicago, Ill.
COOPER, MAUDE EMILY,   Watertown.
CORNELL, CLARA MARGARET,   Asbury Park, N. J.
CROSS, LUCILE,   Fairbury, Neb.
CUMMING, ELLEN KING,   Fredonia.

CURTIS, BESSIE GORDON,	Medford, Mass.
DEANE, EDITH DOUGLAS,	New York.
DENTON, GRACE,	New Hampton.
DEWEY, GERTRUDE A. HUNTINGTON,	St. Albans, Vt.
DICKSON, TENNIE VICTORIA,	Westfield.
DILLOW, PEARL CRYSTAL MARIE,	Cleveland, O.
DOUGLAS, ANNE ELIZABETH,	Indianapolis, Ind.
EDICK, GRACE WILLARD,	Rochester.
EMERY, ETHELYN.	Bryan, O.
FAGAN, JOSEPHINE,	Hackettstown.
FARRAR, ANNIE MARTHA,	Tarboro, N. C.
FERRY, QUEEN,	Detroit, Mich.
FREEMAN, BELLE MARGARET,	Canandaigua.
GETCHELL, HELEN,	Des Moines, Iowa.
GOODSPEED, JESSIE LILLIAN,	Brooklyn.
GRANT, BLANCHE CHLOE,	Indianapolis, Ind.
HAGAR, ALICE PACKARD,	Chicago, Ill.
HART, JESSIE BELL,	Englewood, N. J.
HARTRIDGE, KATHARINE McDONALD,	Savannah, Ga.
HARTZELL, SARAH BRANCH,	Cleveland, O.
HASKELL, FLORENCE AUGUSTA,	Bradford, Pa.
HAWKINS, CAROLINE,	Fall River, Mass.
HAYWARD, ELLEN IMOGENE,	Davenport, Iowa.
HERO, ANNIE,	New Orleans, La.
HEWITT, MARIE DEANE,	Tacoma, Wash.
HIGGINS, MARY ELIZABETH,	Stelton, N. J.
HIGGINS, MEDORA LAMBERT,	Ticonderoga.
HIGMAN, NELLIE,	Sioux City, Ia.
HILL, HELENA CHARLOTTE,	Norwalk, Conn.
HILL, JULIA DELACOUR,	Danbury, Conn.
HOWLAND, ALICE MERRILL,	Hope, R. I.
HULST, ELLA STOOTHOFF,	Brooklyn.
JOHNSON, MIGNONETTE BIRD,	Memphis, Tenn.
JONES, BLANCHE ADALINE,	Pittsburgh, Penn.
JUTTEN, SARA EMMA,	Boston, Mass.
KINKEAD, CORNELIA DODGE,	Poughkeepsie.
KNIGHT, FLORENCE BAILEY,	Chicago, Ill.
KREUSE, IDA GRACE,	Black Hawk, Col.
LAIRD, MARION,	Freehold, N. J.
LOCKHART, LIZZIE MARION,	Mount Vernon.
LORD, ELIZA MARY,	Penn Yan.

Love, Ella Louise,	Chicago, Ill.
Love, Emily,	Memphis, Tenn.
Luehrmann, Adele,	Memphis, Tenn.
Mabie, Muriel Kate,	Boston, Mass.
McAllister, Lillian Angela,	Manchester, N. H.
MacArthur, Gertrude Eugenia,	New York.
McCampbell, Roberta,	Louisville, Ky.
McCloskey, Estelle,	Pittsburgh, Penn.
McFarland, Maude May,	Oswego.
McKean, Ida Paine,	Cleveland, O.
McMillan, Jeannette,	Detroit, Mich.
Madeira, Lucy,	Washington, D. C.
Mann, Ruth Mitchell,	Central Falls, R. I.
Marquardt, Della Mary,	Des Moines, Iowa.
Miller, Alma May,	Winfield, Kan.
Miner, Chastine Mary,	Burlington, Vt.
Moody, Mary Grace,	New Haven, Conn.
Morris, Anna Ruth,	Oregon, Mo.
Morton, Annie,	Fall River, Mass.
Newcomb, May Queen,	Detroit, Mich.
Niles, Bessie Cross,	Springfield, Mass.
O'Brien, Lulu A.,	Penn Yan.
Odell, Anna,	Detroit, Mich.
Paine, Elizabeth,	Paines, Mich.
Palmer, Rose Amelia,	Washington, D. C.
Parkis, Alice Lackey,	North Uxbridge, Mass.
Peckham, Helen Wooster,	Pulaski.
Pellet, Margaret,	Watkins.
Phinney, Lulu Allen,	Alton, Ill.
Pierson, Jessie Durant,	New Haven, Conn.
Reed, Bertha Lavinia,	Ouray, Col.
Reynolds, Kate Beatty,	New Rochelle.
Richardson, Hattie,	Washington, D. C.
Richardson, May Meylert,	Chicago, Ill.
Roberts, Dora Cornelia,	Rochester.
Rudman, Ella May,	Rochester.
Samson, Marian Elizabeth,	Buffalo.
Sanders, Effie Stark,	Springfield, Ill.
Sanders, Mary Noxon,	New York.
Schwartz, Julia Augusta,	Omaha, Neb.
Scott, Florence Bevier,	Philadelphia, Penn.

SCRANTON, HENRIETTE IRENE,	Sault Ste Marie, Mich.
SHEPPARD, LOUISE PATTESON,	Penn Yan.
SILL, ANNA ELIZABETH,	Newark, N. J.
SIMONDS, ETHEL GERTRUDE,	Dayton, O.
SINSABAUGH, HENRIETTA,	Port Jervis,
SPALDING, SARAH GRISWOLD,	Denver, Col.
STONE, ELEANOR MARIA,	Brooklyn.
TARBOX, MARY EDITH,	Fredonia.
THROOP KATHARINE PARKER,	Poughkeepsie.
TOMPKINS, SARA HELENE,	Poughkeepsie.
TRAVER, HOPE,	Memphis, Tenn.
TRYON, GENEVA,	Cambridge, Mass.
TUNNICLIFF, RUTH,	Macomb, Ill.
TUTTLE, ALMA ELIZA,	Hornellsville.
VICKROY, ETTIE LUCILE,	St. Louis, Mo.
WAIT, OLGA ATHENE,	Ithaca.
WARNER, GRACE MAY,	St. Paul, Minn.
WARNER, MAUDE LORAINE,	Cincinnati, O.
WELLINGTON, GRACE ANNA,	Troy.
WELLINGTON, MARJORIE SPAULDING,	Adams, Mass.
WELTON, MABEL ELLA,	Cambridge, Ill.
WEST, CLARA PRAY,	East Braintree, Mass.
WINNINGTON, LAURA,	Brooklyn.
WOOD, HELEN THIRZA,	South Framingham, Mass.
YOUNG, BERTHA KEDZIE,	Hackettstown.

IN SPECIAL COURSES.

ALBRIGHT, CLAUDE ELWOOD,	Albuquerque, N. M.
ARMSTRONG, FANNIE ADELE,	Rome.
BAINBRIDGE, HELEN MAUD,	Rochester.
BEARD, HARRIET ELIZABETH,	Brooklyn.
BEERS, LILA ELIZA,	Chicago, Ill.
BUSH, SUSA LUCILE,	Dubuque, Iowa.
CANDEE, MARION OTIS,	Poughkeepsie.
* CARPENTER, MARY WRIGHT,	Poughkeepsie.
CLAPP, HARRIET BERNHARD,	Fulton.
* CLARKE, ALICE BARNEVELDT,	Poughkeepsie.
DEMAREST, MARY VAN EMBURGH,	Paterson, N. J.
* DOUGHTY, MARY ELENA VAN DEBOGART,	Matteawan.
DUSENBURY, SARAH AUGUSTA,	Troy.
ETHRIDGE, ANNIE STEWART,	Decatur, Ga.

GALLAHER, BESSIE,	Essex, Conn.
GELLER, SOPHRONIA AUSTIN,	Albany.
GREENE, CAROLINE ELIZA,	Providence, R. I.
* HAGGERTY, SUSIE HYDE,	Poughkeepsie.
HAMILTON, FLORENCE ANNA,	West Rush.
HILLIER, EZELU,	Denver, Col.
HULBERT, EDITH JOSEPHINE,	Yonkers.
JARNAGIN, HETTY SHIELDS,	Mossy Creek, Tenn.
LAPHAM, ANNE EDITH,	Canandaigua.
McCLURE, MARY LYON,	Bradford, Penn.
McCURDY, MARY,	Youngstown, O.
MACDONALD, JESSIE LILIAN,	Troy.
MARTIN, ELMA GILLESPIE,	Havana.
MARVIN, ELLEN SUTTON,	Montclair, N. J.
MITCHELL, MERION ELEANOR,	Bay City, Mich.
MOORE, ANNE,	Wilmington, N. C.
MORISSEY, FANNIE ALICE,	Troy.
MULHOLLAND, MARY ESTELLE,	Brockport.
PALMER, GRACE WASHBURN,	Little Falls.
PARMELE, MARY IDA,	Canandaigua.
* PELL, VIRGINIA ISOLIND,	Poughkeepsie.
PERLEY, HARRIET AUGUSTA,	Waverly.
POTTER, MARCIA,	Saginaw, Mich.
REYNOLDS, FLORENCE CLAIRE,	Boone, Iowa.
RISSER, FLORENCE MAE,	Chicago, Ill.
RUSH, DAMARIS,	Columbia City, Ind.
* SANDERS, MAUD LOUISE,	Poughkeepsie.
SCOTT, ELIZABETH GAMBLE,	Lock Haven, Penn.
SHATTUCK, HARRIET COMSTOCK,	Norwich.
SMITH, DELIA,	Boone, Iowa.
STRAIGHT, EDITH JANET,	Bradford, Penn.
THORNTON, LUCY REYNARD,	Fall River, Mass.
TOMPKINS, NANNA MAY,	Poughkeepsie.
* VAN INGEN, JOSEPHINE KOELMAN,	Poughkeepsie.
WAGNER, MARY SWAIN,	Minneapolis, Minn.
WALDRON, FRANCES EDITH,	Poughkeepsie.
* WIETHAN, MAY JOSEPHINE,	Poughkeepsie.
WORTHINGTON, ALICE LOUISE,	Hartford, Conn.

* Students studying music or painting only.
In December, 1891, the Trustees abolished the special schools, but continued the old courses of work for those already entered. For the new regulations regarding these arts see p 28.

SUMMARY.

Graduate Students, ...	3
Seniors, ...	53
Juniors, ...	71
Sophomores, ...	111
Freshmen, ...	140
In Special Courses, ...	52

Whole number, ...	430

ADMISSION OF STUDENTS.

REQUIREMENTS FOR ADMISSION TO THE FRESH-MAN CLASS.

Applicants for admission to the Freshman or any higher class must be at least sixteen years of age. They must present satisfactory testimonials of good character.

Candidates for the Freshman Class are examined in the following studies :

English : Every candidate will be required to write an essay of from three to five pages upon a subject assigned at the time, and taken from one of the following works :

Shakspere's Julius Cæsar and Twelfth Night; Scott's Marmion ; Longfellow's Courtship of Miles Standish ; Addison's Sir Roger de Coverly Papers ; Macaulay's second Essay on the Earl of Chatham ; Emerson's American Scholar ; Irving's Sketch Book ; Scott's Ivanhoe ; Dicken's David Copperfield.

This essay must be correct in spelling, punctuation, grammar, structure of paragraphs, and rhetorical expression.

In 1894 the subjects will be taken from the following works :

Shakspere's Julius Cæsar and Merchant of Venice ; Scott's Lady of the Lake; Arnold's Sohrab and Rustrum ; The Sir Roger de Coverly Papers in the "Spectator;" Macaulay's second Essay on the Earl of Chatham ; Emerson's American Scholar ; Irving's Sketch Book ; Scott's Abbot ; Dicken's David Copperfield.

In 1895 : Shakspere's Merchant of Venice and Twelfth Night; Milton's L'Allegro. Ii Penseroso. Comus, and Lycidas ; Longfellow's Evangeline ; The Sir Roger de Coverly Papers in the "Spectator ; " Macaulay's Essays on Milton and Addison ; Webster's first Bunker Hill Oration ; Irving's Sketch Book ; Scott's Abbot.

Candidates will also be required to correct specimens of bad English furnished at the time. (Strang's Exercises in English recommended.)

History : Outlines of Greek and Roman history to the establish-ment of the Roman Empire; outlines of American or English history. Any standard history of Greece, Rome, England, or the United States may be used. The following are recommended : For Greek and Roman history, Pennell's Ancient Greece and Pennell's Ancient Rome, or the sections on Greek and Roman history in Sheldon's General History or Myers' General History ; for American history. Johnston's History of the United States, or Montgomery's Leading Facts in American History ; for English history, Gardiner's English History for Schools or Montgomery's Leading Facts in English History.

Mathematics: (a) Arithmetic, including the metric system of weights and measures, as much as is contained in the larger text-books.

(b) Algebra.—The requirements in Algebra embrace the following subjects : Factors ; Common Divisors and Multiples ; Fractions ; Ratio and Proportion.; Negative Quantities and Interpretation of Negative Results ; The Doctrine of Exponents ; Radicals and Equations involving Radicals ; The Binomial Theorem and the Extraction of Roots ; Arithmetical and Geometrical Progressions ; Putting Questions into Equations ; The ordinary methods of Elimination and the solution of both Numerical and Literal Equations of the First and Second Degrees, with one or more unknown quantities, and of problems leading to such equations. The text-books used should be equivalent to the larger treatises of Newcomb, Olney, Ray, Robinson, Todhunter, Wells or Wentworth.

(c) Plane geometry, as much as is contained in the first five books of Chauvenet's Treatise on Elementary Geometry, or the first five books of Wentworth's New Plane and Solid Geometry. or Wells' Plane Geometry, or the first six books of Hamblin Smith's Elements of Geometry, or chapter first of Olney's Elements of Geometry. In order to pursue successfully the work of the College, ·recent review of the work completed early in the preparatory course is neccessary.

Latin : Grammar (Allen & Greenough preferred) ; Latin Composition, Collar (Parts third and fourth), or Daniell (Parts first and second , or Allen (50 lessons) ; Cæsar, Gallic War, four books ; Cicero, seven orations (the Manilian Law to count as two); Vergil, *Æneid,* six books. The Eclogues will be accepted as an equivalent for an oration of Cicero, or one of the six books of the Æneid. Translation at sight from Cæsar and Cicero's orations. The Roman method of pronunciation is used.

The attention of preparatory schools is called to the advantage of accustoming the student to the Roman method of pronunciation from the beginning, to the need of greater practical regard for the value of vowel quantities, and the training of the ear by familiarizing the student with the sound of the language.

IN ADDITION TO THE LATIN ONE OTHER LANGUAGE IS REQUIRED. This may be Greek, German, or French.

Greek: Grammar; Woodruff, *Greek Prose Composition.* White, *The Beginner's Greek Book,* or Harper, *Inductive Greek Method;* Xenophon, *Anabasis,* four books; Homer, *Iliad,* three books. Translation at sight of average passages from Zenophon's *Anabasis* and Homer's *Iliad,* and of English into Greek.

German: Candidates for the Freshman class are expected to have a thorough knowledge of German grammar; they must have acquired facility in practically applying the rules of construction by translating easy English prose into German. They are also required to read and to be able to give in German some account of the following works: Immermann, *Der Oberhof;* Wagner, *Goethe's Knabenjahre* (Cambridge University Press ed.); Lessing, *Minna von Barnhelm;* Schiller, *Wilhelm Tell;* Goethe, *Hermann und Dorothea;* Freytag, *Die Journalisten.*

Throughout the course German is the language of the class-room, therefore good preparation in conversation is necessary, facility in reading and writing German script indispensable.

French: A thorough knowledge of French Grammar and ability to translate easy English prose into French. (Whitney, *Practical French Grammar,* recommended). Six of Bocher's College Plays; Daudet, *La Belle Nivernaise;* Souvestre, *Un Philosophe Sous Les Toits;* Julliot, *Mademoiselle Solange;* Dumas, *La Tulipe Noire;* Erckmann-Chatrian, *Le Conscrit de 1813.*

As French is the language of the class-room, it is desirable that candidates for admission should have some practice in French conversation.

The full preparation in either French or German should cover a period of at least two years, five recitations a week, under competent instructors.

EXAMINATIONS.

Examinations for admission to the Freshman Class will be held at the College, Thursday, Friday and Saturday preceding Commencement, June 8, 9, and 10, 1893 ; also, if early application is made, at Chicago, Cincinnati, Cleveland, St. Louis, Detroit, Louisville, Atlanta, Washington, Omaha, Denver, and San Francisco, during the first week in June, 1893.

Applicants for examination at any of these places must inform the President before the first day of May, and they will be duly notified of the day and place.

The regular examinations at the College for the admission of students will commence on Wednesday, September 20, 1893, and continue three days.

Candidates are requested to be present at 9 A. M. for registration.

The order of entrance examinations is as follows : ·

First Day,   Latin, 9.30 A. M. to 12 M.
            English, 2 P. M. to 4:30 P. M.
Second Day, Algebra and Geometry, 9.30 A. M. to 12 M.
            History, 2 P. M. to 4:30 P. M.
Third Day, Greek, German, and French, 9:30 A. M. to 12 M.
            Arithmetic, 2 P. M. to 3:30 P. M.

Students cannot have rooms at the college until their examinations have been completed. Lodging may be procured at cottages near the College upon application to the Registrar.

Students entering on certificate should not present themselves until Thursday of examination week.

CERTIFICATES.

Students are admitted without examinations in the following cases :

1. When they bring a certificate of proficiency from schools from which a pupil has previously been admitted without condition to the Freshman or a higher class.

2. When they have been prepared by a graduate of the College engaged in the work of private instruction, one of whose pupils has

before been admitted without condition to the Freshman òr a higher class.

3.   When they bring certificates from schools which have been visited by a committee of the Faculty and approved by them, or in regard to which the Faculty have other sufficient means of information.

The College reserves to itself the right to withdraw the above mentioned privilege in case students thus admitted fail after fair trial to maintain their standing.

4.   The certificate of the Regents of the State of New York will be accepted in place of examination, so far as it meets the requirements for admission to the College.

5.   The certificate of the president of Harvard College, offered by persons who have successfully passed " the examinations for women," so far as it includes studies, preparatory or collegiate, prescribed in the regular course, will be accepted in lieu of examination in such studies.

In all cases the certificate must specify the text-book used, the ground actually gone over, and the date of examination. Blank forms will be furnished by the President on application.

All certificates must be based upon recent examinations.

They must be forwarded to the College early in the summer.

SPECIAL COURSES.

The requirements for admission to special courses are the same as those for entrance to the Freshman class. Candidates must consult the President in regard to the desired courses of study, and in connection with the heads of the departments which they may wish to enter, he will arrange their work.

PAINTING AND MUSIC.

The special schools heretofore existing have been abolished. Professorships of Music and Painting have been established, and the history and theory of the arts have been placed on a level with other college work as counting toward the Baccalaureate degree.

The College also provides instruction in the practice of the arts, but for this extra charge is made. This work is not counted toward the degree.

These courses are open to regular and special students alike, but no one may enter them who is not prepared for the Freshman year. The design of the Trustees is to recognize the true place of these studies in higher education. They will provide the fullest facilities for those who are able to meet the requirements of the College for admission.

COURSES FOR TEACHERS.

Teachers who desire to pursue special courses and who present to the President satisfactory testimonials of their success in teaching and of their proficiency as students may be received without examination. Certificates of the work accomplished will be given when desired.

ADMISSION TO ADVANCED STANDING.

Candidates for advanced standing, not coming from other colleges, may be admitted, on examination, to the regular course at any time previous to the beginning of the Junior year. Such students will be examined in all *prescribed* studies antecedent to the desired grade, including the requirements for admission to the College, and in such *elective* studies as shall be chosen by the candidate and approved by the Faculty.

Candidates coming from other colleges must submit their courses of study and their certificates to the judgment of the Faculty. No student will be received as a candidate for the degree of Bachelor of Arts after the beginning of the Senior year.

COURSES AND METHODS OF INSTRUCTION.

ARRANGED BY DEPARTMENTS.

The course of study leading to the Baccalaureate Degree extends over four years.

The curriculum has been carefully formed with regard to the conflicts between the Prescribed and Elective Systems, and with the belief that experience demonstrates the need of much careful compulsory work as a preparation for free choice.

The aim is to give the student the opportunity to follow lines of study continuously, through both the required and optional portions of the course.

All elections are subject to the approval of the Faculty.

Two languages, one of which shall be Latin, must be studied throughout the *prescribed* course by every student for a degree. The second language may be Greek, German, or French.

An opportunity is given, in the elective part of the course, for beginning the study of Greek, German, or French.

LATIN.

ASSOCIATE PROFESSOR MOORE, MISS GREENE AND MISS BERRY.

The course in Latin extends through the four years of the undergraduate course, being required for the first two and elective for the last two years. The aim of the course is to acquaint the student with the principal phases of literary activity among the Romans through the study of representative authors. In the department of History Livy and Tacitus exhibit natural development in style and method. Cicero and Lucretius represent opposing schools in Roman Philosophy ; Horace and Juvenal show the growth of Satire ; Horace, Catullus and Propertius that of the elegy and the lyric, Plautus and

Terence the course of Roman Comedy. The letters of Cicero and Pliny together present the every-day side of Roman life and language. Using these authors as starting-points the endeavor is to bring before the student the lines along which the various departments developed, and also to show the connection of literature with history and politics, as well as with the various social conditions and relations of Roman life.

The development of the language into its literary form is pointed out through explanations of grammatical forms and constructions, and the relation in which these stand to the historical-growth of syntax. Much stress is laid on these points in connection with the required work of the Freshman and Sophomore years, and while attention is still directed towards them in the elective courses of the Junior and Senior years (especially in the study of Plautus and Terence), the literary side of the language is made prominent. Facility in reading Latin is cultivated by translation at sight in connection with the prose authors of the required part of the course as well as with the elective courses of the upper years. The study of Latin Composition is pursued in the Freshman and Sophomore years for the most part in connection with the authors read.

REQUIRED.

1. Livy, Books XXI and XXII (*Westcott*) [3], Latin Prose Composition [1]. Freshman year, first semester.

MISS GREENE AND MISS BERRY.

The principal object of this course is to enable the student to read Latin with greater rapidity, intelligence and appreciation. As a means to this end frequent exercises in Latin composition, based on the text, and translation from hearing form regular class exercises. The peculiarities of Livy's style are carefully noted and compared with the classic idiom.

2. Horace, Odes (*Wickham*) [3], Latin Prose Composition [1]. Freshman year, second semester.

MISS GREENE AND MISS BERRY.

The Odes of Horace are considered from a literary rather than a linguistic point of view. The work includes criticism of form and style and analysis of the thought, with a certain amount of collateral reading. The course in Prose Composition continues and supplements the work of the first semester.

3. Cicero, De Senectute, De Amicitia (*Kelsey*) [2], Latin Prose Composition [1]. Sophomore year, first semester.

DR. MOORE, MISS GREENE AND MISS BERRY.

In this course the student is led to trace carefully the development and connection of thought in the essays read, and to acquire a knowledge of Roman Stoicism as set forth by Cicero. The Latin Prose course is of a more advanced character and deals with questions of style and form as well as correctness of expression. Special attention is given to the correction and discussion of exercises privately prepared by the student.

4. Horace, Satires and Epistles (*Greenough*) [2]. Sophomore year, second semester.   MISS GREENE AND MISS BERRY.

Those Satires and Epistles are read which bear on some special subject; *e. g.* Horace's defense of his literary position, his criticism of Lucilius, his portrayal of life and society in Rome, his relations with Maecenas. Peculiarities of syntax and diction are noted, especially those which show the influence of the vulgar idiom.

ELECTIVE.

Course A. Ovid, Fasti, Book VI (*Sidgwick*), Lucan, Pharsalia, Book I (*Heitland & Haskins*) [2]. Sophomore year, second semester.
DR. MOORE.

The course aims to exhibit in a general way the development of the Elegy and the Epic under the Early Empire.

Course B. Roman Comedy, Terence, Andria (*Freeman and Sloman*) [3]. First semester.   DR. MOORE.

Besides the play mentioned, characteristic passages from plays of Plautus and Terence are translated at sight in class and the work is further supplemented by lectures on Roman comedy and the preparation of special papers by the class.

Course C. Tacitus, Agricola or Germania (*Allen*), Annals (*Allen*) [3]. Second semester.   DR. MOORE.

On the linguistic side the syntax and style of Tacitus are studied as introducing the student to the characteristics of the Silver Age of Latin prose. Collateral reading on the period covered, and lectures on the historians between Livy and Tacitus are included in the course.

Course D. Roman Elegy, Catullus, Propertius and Tibullus [3]. First semester.   DR. MOORE.

Catullus' position among Latin poets, his originality, the effect upon him of the Alexandrine school and similar questions will be specially considered. Propertius and Tibullus will be used to illustrate the development of the elegy.

This course will be given in 1893–4.

Course E. Juvenal, Satires (*Hardy*), Pliny, Letters (*Prichard and Bernard*) [3]. First semester.   DR. MOORE.

As these authors present opposite views of social life in Rome under the Early Empire, an important feature of the work consists in the preparation of papers on various topics suggested by the text.

Course F. Lucretius (*Kelsey*), Cicero, De Natura Deorum (*Stickney*) [3]. Second semester.   DR. MOORE.

The presentation and criticism of the Stoic and Epicurean philosophies, as set forth in these authors, are compared with theories of modern science and the work is supplemented by collateral reading. The style and language of Lucretius are also considered.

SANSKRIT.
DR. MOORE.

Sanskrit is a two-hour elective course in Senior year. Students are requested to consult with the instructor before electing it.

Course A.—Study of the characters, sounds, roots and inflections of Sanskrit; first semester [2]. *Perry*, Primer; *Whitney*, Grammar.

Course B.—Reading of selections from the Nalopākhyānam and the Hitopadeça ; second semester [2]. *Perry*, Primer (finished); *Lanman*, Reader ; *Whitney*, Grammar.

GREEK.
PROFESSOR LEACH AND MISS GREENE.

The aim is to acquire as many-sided a knowledge of Greek as possible. Facility in reading Greek is cultivated, and to this end, practice at sight is given and private reading is encouraged. Attention is paid to grammatical principles, to the development of the language and of the literature, to different phases of Greek life and thought. Careful study is given to the style of each author and to the distinctive excellence of each, and in advanced classes, to text-criticism. The courses given embrace representative authors in history, oratory, philosophy, in epic, lyric, and dramatic poetry. In the Junior year, a course in elementary Greek is offered to any non-Greek students who may wish it. Such students have an opportunity to continue the work with the subsequent Freshman class.

REQUIRED.

1. Lysias ; Plato, *Phaedrus* [3]. English into Greek [1]: Translation at sight and also from hearing. Lectures on legal, political, and social aspects of Athenian life. Freshman year, first semester.
PROFESSOR LEACH AND MISS GREENE.

2. Homer, *Odyssey ;* Herodotus [3]. English into Greek [1]. Translation at sight. Lectures on Homeric Antiquities and on the Homeric Question. Historical explanation of the Homeric Forms and Syntax. Freshman year, second semester.
PROFESSOR LEACH AND MISS GREENE.

3. Selections from the *Attic Orators* [2]. English into Greek [1] Lectures on Attic Orators. Sophomore year, first semester.
PROFESSOR LEACH.

4. Plato, *Protagoras* ; Aristophanes, *Clouds* [2]. Lectures on Socrates, the Socratic Method, the Sophists, the wit and humor of Aristophanes, the language of Comedy. Sophomore year, second semester.
PROFESSOR LEACH.

ELECTIVE.

Course A. (Short course) Grammar, *Anabasis, Iliad* [3]. First and second semesters.
PROFESSOR LEACH.

Course B. Thucydides, Book II [2]. Lectures on the Age of Pericles, on the Greek Historians, on the style and language of Thucydides. First semester.
PROFESSOR LEACH.

Course C. Sophocles, *Œdipus at Colonus.* Euripides, *Hippolytus* [3]. Lectures on the Attic Theatre and the Drama, on Athens and its Monuments. Second semester.
PROFESSOR LEACH.

Course D. Pindar, *Olympian and Pythian Odes* [2]. Lectures on the Lyric Poets and on the discoveries at Olympia. First semester.
PROFESSOR LEACH.

Course E. Plato, *Republic* ; Aristotle, *Nicomachean Ethics* [3]. Lectures on Greek Philosophy. Second semester.
PROFESSOR LEACH.

A society, called the Hellenic Society, has been formed for the purpose of keeping itself acquainted with the results of archæological research in Greece.

Vassar College now contributes to the support of the American School of Classical Studies at Athens. The school affords facilities for archæological investigation and study in Greece, and graduates of this college are entitled to all its advantages without expense for tuition.

FRENCH.

PROFESSOR BRACQ AND MISS EPLER.

The aim of this course is three-fold: 1st. To give a correct knowledge of the French language and of its evolution from the Latin tongue. During the first year, the most important principles of grammar are reviewed. Throughout the course, constant attention is given to their application during both the reading and the conversational exercises. The study of the first year is grammatical, that of the second is grammatical and philological. 2d. To enable the student to speak the language fluently. To this end great efforts are made to educate the ear and to secure fluency of speech. The text-books are French. The answers of the students, the lectures and discussions are all in French. 3d. To give a philosophical knowledge of French literature, its origin, its development, its master-pieces, its pictures of French society at different periods; in other words, French history as seen in French literature. Special efforts are made to enable the student to grasp the modern thought and life of France in their literary manifestations.

The course in Old French is intended to furnish a basis both for the study of Early English and the historical study of the French language, and at the same time to enable the student to read with facility the early productions of the Langue d'Oïl. The most remarkable specimen of that literature of Northern France, *La Chanson de Roland*, is read in class.

The Short Course is designed for students who wish to be able to read French with ease, and to understand French conversation: The work includes the study of grammar, prose composition, and the reading of modern prose.

REQUIRED.

1 and 2. Lamartine, *Graziella*, Hugo, *Hernani* and *La Chûte*, Super's Readings from French History and Bowen's French Lyrics. Review of Syntax. Translation of English into French. Exercises in conversation. One hour a week of the second semester is devoted to the French literature of the nineteenth century [4]. Freshman year, first and second semesters.

PROFESSOR BRACQ AND MISS EPLER.

3. The study of the literature of the nineteenth century continued. Reading of extracts from the works of Cousin, Sainte-Beuve, Paul Bourget and Taine. As the students do not begin the study of the French of the eighteenth or of the seventeeth century until they are grounded in contemporary French, the confusion that arises by not keeping the periods distinct is avoided. Twelve lectures are given upon the history of the French language [3]. Sophomore year, first semester. PROFESSOR BRACQ.

4. Montesquieu. *Considérations sur les causes de la grandeur des Romains et leur décadence*, Bernardin de Saint Pierre, *Paul et Virginie*. Voltarie, *Mérope*. Lectures upon the literature of the eighteenth century and upon its relations to the French Revolution. Conversation [2]. Sophomore year, second semester.

PROFESSOR BRACQ.

ELECTIVE.

Course A. Short Course. Principles of grammar. Hennequin's Verbs, Paul Bercy, *La Langue française*. Reading, Henry Gréville, *Perdue*, Madame de Presseusé, *Rosa*, Scribe, *Les Doigts de fée*, Halévy, *Un marriage d'amour*. Prose composition and conversation [3]. First and second semesters. MISS EPLER.

Course B. Old French. Introductory lectures to the study of Old French. Brief survey of grammatical principles. The Norman-French element in the English Language. Reading of *La Chanson de Roland* [2]. First semester. PROFESSOR BRACQ.

Course C. Corneille, *Le Cid*, Racine, *Andromaque*, Molière, *Le Bourgeois gentilhomme*. Lectures upon the society of the XVIIth century, the Hotel de Rambouillet and the French Academy. Discussions of topics that have been prepared by the students. Conversation [2]. First semester. PROFESSOR BRACQ.

Course D. Critical, analytical, and comparative study of the drama of the seventeenth century. Lectures upon the rise of the French drama. Extensive readings. Conversation [2]. Second semester.

PROFESSOR BRACQ.

Course E. The philosophical, the religious, and the miscellaneous literature of the seventeenth century, Pascal, Descartes, Bossuet, La Fontaine and Mme. de Sévigné. Lectures and conversation [2]. First semester. PROFESSOR BRACQ.

Course F. Reading of extracts from the works of Amyot, Montaigne, Pascal and other writers of the Renaissance period. Lec-

tures on French literature from its beginning to our times ; its in-
fluence upon other literatures ; its best modern representatives in
France, Switzerland, Belgium, and Canada [2].   Second semester.
PROFESSOR BRACQ.

GERMAN.

ASSOCIATE PROFESSOR HERHOLZ AND MISS NEEF.

The aim of the German course is to give the students a thorough
knowledge of the language, so as to enable them to pursue the study
of history and the sciences with German text-books, and to understand and appreciate to the fullest extent the productions of literature.
It is also intended to give them the ability to use the language con-
versationally with the greatest possible accuracy and freedom.

In the Freshman year the grammatical principles are carefully reviewed and in the subsequent classes incidental instruction in grammar is given.

The History of Literature is begun in the first semester of the
Sophomore year and continued in every following semester, with lectures on the most prominent authors and their works.   This course
embraces the development of language and literature from the earliest
stages down to the present day and is calculated to give the student
a clear conception of the great epochs in the literary evolution of Ger-
many.

REQUIRED.

1 and 2. Grammar. Composition. Special attention is given to
translation at sight from English into German.   Selections from
Harris, German composition. Hoffman, *Historische Erzahlungen;*
Auerbach, *Joseph und Benjamin.*   Poems by Goethe, Schiller, Uhland,
Chamisso, etc.   Schiller, *Maria Stuart* or Goethe, *Egmont* [4].
Freshman year, first and second semesters.
ASSOCIATE PROFESSOR HERHOLZ AND MISS NEEF.

3. History of Literature from the early beginning to the eighteenth century.   Selections from the first classical period. Schiller,
Wallenstein ; Lessing, *Emilia Galotti.* Composition [3]. Sophomore
year, first semester.   MISS NEEF.

4. The work of the first semester continued [2].   Sophomore year,
second semester.   MISS NEEF.

ELECTIVE.

Course A. Wenckebach and Schrakamp, Grammar. Joynes. *German Reader ;* Storm, *Immensee ;* Lessing, *Minna von Barnhelm* [3].
First and second semesters.   ASSOCIATE PROFESSOR HERHOLZ.

This short course is intended to give mature students an opportunity to begin the study of German and to acquire a practical knowledge of the language.

The work consists of a thorough drill in grammar, with written and oral exercises, translation from German into English and vice versa, and of reading and memorizing prose and poetry, the matter read being made the subject of conversation and composition. Great attention is paid to pronunciation and correct expression.

Course B. History of Literature of the XVIII century. Discussion of the influence of authors on their contemporaries and entire periods. Schiller, *Braut von Messina.* Essays upon topics suggested by the class-work [2]. First semester.

ASSOCIATE PROFESSOR HERHOLZ.

Students are expected to read extracts from the histories of German literature by different authors, to study the lives of the great poets in connection with their works and with the political, social, and intellectual movements of their times.

Course C. History of Literature of the XVIII century and work of Course B continued. Goethe, *Iphigenie, Tasso ;* Lessing, *Nathan* [2]. Second semester.   ASSOCIATE PROFESSOR HERHOLZ.

Course D. History of modern Literature. Critical study of poetical productions. Collateral readings and lectures will supplement the work in the class-room. Essays. Lessing's Prose works [2]. First semester.   ASSOCIATE PROFESSOR HERHOLZ.

Course E. Work of Course D continued. Goethe, *Faust*, Parts I and II [2]. Second semester.   ASSOCIATE PROFESSOR HERHOLZ.

ENGLISH.

PROFESSOR DRENNAN, MISS PERRY, DR. SWEET, MISS LOOMIS.

The instruction in English includes the three departments of Rhetoric and Composition, English Literature, and Anglo-Saxon. There is also a short course of lectures on English Philology. During the first two years the work is all prescribed, in the Junior and Senior years, elective.

The aim in Rhetoric and English Composition is to enable the student to acquire facility, correctness, and clearness in writing English. With this in view the instruction during the first two years is combined with that in Literature, and these two courses are correlated, and conducted so that one shall illustrate the other. A number of essays on simple subjects are required, and also frequent exercises in extempore writing; there is besides instruction in the art of taking notes, making abstracts, etc., etc   Several carefully prepared essays are also demanded : these are closely criticised in a personal interview with the student.   There is continued practice in off-hand writing in reporting discourses and in making abstracts of authors read, subjects assigned, etc.

REQUIRED.

1 and 2.   Rhetoric and Literature [3].   Freshman year, first and second semesters.   MISS PERRY AND MISS LOOMIS.

3 and 4.   Literature [2].   Rhetoric [1].   Sophomore year, first and second semesters.   MISS SWEET AND MISS PERRY.

The Rhetoric of the Freshman year begins with Narrative and Descriptive Composition ; after Thanksgiving the principles of Analysis, Structure of the Essay, Sermon, and Lecture are taken up in conjunction with practice in making abstracts of discourses.   In the Sophomore it is a continuation and enlargement of the work of the previous year.   The fundamental principles of style are discussed in the class-room.   Short themes, embodying these principles, are then written extempore and submitted to general discussion and criticism. Short themes, as well as longer essays, written outside the class-room, are subjected to private criticism.

The Literature begins the first semester of the Freshman year and the aim is to make the student see what is meant by the study of Literature as opposed to cursory and accidental reading.   Popular and influential authors are chosen, and the student is urged to discover if she may the causes of their success.   Several masterpieces in prose are critically read and the instruction combined with that in Rhetoric. In the second semester selections from eminent recent poets are carefully studied.

During the Sophomore year the work begins with the especial study of some great writer—his works, life, school, influence, etc.   In 1892-'93 Wordsworth was thus treated.   For the remainder of the year the course consists of a survey of English Literature in its formative period beginning with Wycliffe.   The student is expected to become acquainted with the various authors at first hand : the earlier ones by means of specimens ; the later ones by means of more or less copious extracts, or, in some instances, of entire works.

Course A. Advanced Rhetoric. Consisting of lectures, collateral reading, and essays [2]. First semester. MISS PERRY.

The lectures include a treatment of the principles of literary criticism, supplemented by assigned library work. For the second semester a course in essays is offered. The essays of this year as well as those of preceding years are discussed in private interviews with the instructor.

Course B. Essays [1]. Second semester. MISS PERRY.

This course is intended for those who wish further instruction and practice in composition.

Course C. Forensics. A course in argumentative essays, instruction in controversial writing, open only to those who have taken logic and course A [2]. First semester. MISS PERRY.

Course D. Shakspere; Laws of Dramatic Composition; Lectures [3]. First semester. PROFESSOR DRENNAN.

The purpose of this course is to give an introduction to the various lines of Shakspere study, historical, literary, philological. A single play is thoroughly mastered, and the student is then assisted to draw out analytically the laws of dramatic poetry. A few other plays, if possible one of each class, are similarly treated.

Course E. English Literature: Period of Queene Anne [3]. Second semester. PROFESSOR DRENNAN.

This course includes a thorough study of the three great writers of the period, Addison, Swift, and Pope, and also a survey of the social, political, ecclesiastical, literary, and physical forces which render this age important.

Courses F. and *G.* Anglo-Saxon. Sweet's Reader with supplementary lessons on the Phonology. [3] First semester; [2] second semester. PROFESSOR DRENNAN.

It is believed that this is sufficient to give the student a good basis for future Anglo-Saxon and Old English studies.

Course H. English Literature. Chaucer [2]. First semester. PROFESSOR DRENNAN.

After the grammatical forms and glossary are mastered, selections from the various works of the author are critically read; attention is also given to the literary history of the period.

Course I. English Philology. This course consists of a series of lectures, designed to give the student some notion of the nature and scope of the science of language. Supplementary readings are required in Max Müller's work, in Prof. Whitney's " Life and Growth of Language," Earle's " Philology of the English Tongue," Lounsbury's " History of the English Language," and in several other similar works [1]. Second semester.   PROFESSOR DRENNAN.

MATHEMATICS.

PROFESSOR ELY AND MISS RICHARDSON.

The courses are divided into two classes, prescribed and elective. The prescribed courses comprise a year and a half of Solid Geometry, Algebra and Trigonometry. These are supplemented by elective courses in Analytic Geometry, Plane and Solid, and in Calculus.

The aim in all the courses is to cultivate habits of exact, sustained and independent reasoning, of precision and clearness in the statement of convictions and the reasons upon which they depend ; to rely upon insight, originality and judgment rather than upon memory. .The endeavor is to secure full possession of leading principles and methods rather than of details. From the first, students who show special aptitude are encouraged in the working of subjects which require more prolonged investigation than the daily exercise of the class-room.

1. Solid and Spherical Geometry [3]. Freshman year, first semester.
2. Algebra [3]. Freshman year, second semester.

MISS RICHARDSON.

The exercises in Geometry include recitations from the text book, original demonstrations of propositions and applications of principles to numerical examples. The text book is Chauvenet (new edition).

The text book in Algebra is Hall and Knight's Higher Algebra.

3. Plane and Spherical Trigonometry [3]. Sophomore year, first semester.   PROFESSOR ELY.

In Plane Trigonometry attention is given to Trigonometric analysis and the solution of triangles. After the student has gained facility in the use of Trigonometric tables, applications of the principles are made to problems in Mensuration, Surveying and Navigation. Up to December attention is given to problems of heights, distances, and areas and to the fundamental principles of Navigation. Afterward the time is devoted to Spherical Trigonometry and its applications to the elementary problems relating to the celestial sphere and to navigation.

Course A. Analytic Geometry (Bowser) [4]. Sophomore year, second semester.　　　　　PROFESSOR ELY.

In Analytic Geometry the student is carried through the elementary properties of lines and surfaces of the second degree. All principles are illustrated by numerous exercises and applications.

Course B. Differential Calculus (Osborne) [3]. First semester.

Course C. Integral Calculus (Osborne) [3]. Second semester.
　　　　　PROFESSOR ELY.

The elective course in Differential and Integral Calculus is designed for those who wish to pursue the subject of either pure or applied Mathematics. The text-book forms the basis of work but is largely supplemented by oral instruction.

This course presupposes Course A.

Course D. Differential and Integral Calculus or Extended Course in Analytic Geometry [3]. First semester.　　PROFESSOR ELY.

Two courses are open to the student, one an extension of the Analytic Geometry of the Sophomore year, including the use of determinants and Tri-linear Co-ordinates. The other continuing the work of the previous semester is an extended course in Calculus, based on Williamson's text-books, and includes the elements of theory of functions of imaginary variables, the various methods of integration systematically treated, differential equations.

Course E. Quaternions [3]. Second semester. PROFESSOR ELY.

This course includes the general properties of scalars and vectors, Quaternion interpretation and applications of Quaternions to the Geometry of the plane, right-line and sphere.

Course E presupposes Courses A and B.

Astronomy.

PROFESSOR WHITNEY.

The courses in Astronomy are all elective. Their leading aim is to acquaint the student with the methods of investigation by which Astronomy has reached its present status, and to give such practice in these methods as the previous attainment of the classes and the appliances of the observatory will allow.

Course A. Descriptive and Historical [1]. First semester.

This lecture course is open to all students. It is intended for those of literary tastes who may desire an outline knowledge of Astronomy without entering upon its scientific treatment. It is not essential to the courses which follow in the schedule, nor is it recommended to those proposing to study Astronomy as a science.

Course B. General Astronomy [3]. First semester.

Course C. General Astronomy (continued) [3]. Second semester.

The course in General Astronomy runs through the year. It provides an elementary but scientific treatment of the principal departments of Astronomy, and is illustrated by frequent examples and applications, drawn as far as possible from local data. It presupposes the required mathematics of the College curriculum, and is also of value to the student as a course in applied mathematics. The students have the free use of the portable telescopes, and such questions as they can determine by their own observations with these glasses are kept before them.

Course D. Spherical and Practical Astronomy [3]. First semester.

Course E. Theoretical Astronomy [2]. Second semester.

These courses enter into a more detailed study of certain departments of Practical and Theoretical Astronomy, and require a working knowledge of the Calculus. They must, therefore, presuppose Mathematical courses A and B. During the first semester the students use the meridian circle, making and reducing their own observations. They predict occulations and observe them. In the second semester practice is transferred to the equatorial telescope and micrometric measurements. The order and character of practical work through the year, however, must frequently vary according to the positions of celestial objects of study. Theoretical Astronomy is generally treated under the form of Comet's orbit.

Course F. Solar Physics [2]. Second semester.

The course in Solar Physics will introduce the student to the principles underlying the study of the constitution of the celestial bodies by the spectroscope, especially in their application to the sun. This course does not presuppose the course in General Astronomy, but an ordinary knowledge of the Solar System is desirable.

PHYSICS.

PROFESSOR COOLEY.

The complete course in Physics extends through four semesters, beginning with the Junior year. The first two semesters are devoted to the study of the general principles of the several branches of the science, viz : Matter and Energy, Phenomena of Solids, Liquids and

Gases, Heat, Sound, Light and Electricity. The two semesters of the Senior year are given to the practical study of selected branches in detail.

In General Physics the first semester is given to the study of the following subjects; the properties of matter, force, energy, special phenomena in solids, liquids and gases, heat and magnetism.

The second semester is given to the study of molecular and radiant energy, including the phenomena of sound, light and electricity.

Lectures, amply illustrated by experiments, introduce the various subjects and give an outline of the plan of study. With this preparation the student passes to the library to pursue a course of reading covering the ground marked out. A general discussion of the subject in the class-room follows this lecture and library work, and, finally, a semi-annual examination completes the work of each semester.

In Practical Physics laboratory work is involved. These courses are expected to enable the student to become more thoroughly acquainted with the facts and principles of special subjects, with the construction and use of instruments, and with the experimental methods of research.

The cabinet of physical apparatus is well supplied with instruments suited to the work of the lecture room, and with many others adapted to the exact work of the laboratory. Constant additions of modern instruments are being made. A special fund for this purpose permits the purchase of apparatus from the best American and European makers, as needed.

ELECTIVE.

Course A. General Physics; Matter and Energy, Phenomena of solids and fluids, Heat, Magnetism [4]. First semester.

Course B. General Physics; Sound, Light, Electricity [3]. Second semester.

Course C. Practical Physics; Experimental work in Physical Measurements and Electricity with lectures and collateral reading [3]. First semester.

Course D. Practical Physics; Experimental work in Light with lectures and collateral reading [3]. Second semester.

Courses C and D will be open to those who, having taken Courses A and B, desire to study one or two branches in detail and to become acquainted with experimental methods in Physics.

CHEMISTRY.

PROFESSOR COOLEY, ASSOCIATE PROFESSOR MOULTON, AND MISS FREEMAN.

The course in chemistry consists of four exercises weekly during four semesters and an additional two hours weekly in one semester. The object of this course is to acquaint the student with the experimental method of research, and to enable her to acquire by this method a thorough and systematic knowledge of the elementary facts and principles of chemistry.

Instruction is given by means of lectures which are supplemented by laboratory investigation, library study, general discussion in the class-room, and semi-annual examinations.

The general character of the work done and the special object sought in each semester may be stated as follows : The first semester is devoted to a study of the non-metals and their compounds. In this " first course " the student is expected to acquire some skill in manipulation. She is taught how to bring about various forms of chemical changes, how to investigate a chemical action by separating and identifying its products, and she is shown how the laws of combination and other principles of the science are obtained by generalizing the results of experimental work.

The second semester is devoted to a study of the metals and their compounds. In this " second course " the student is expected to become acquainted with the properties of the most typical and useful metals and to make a systematic laboratory study of their reactions. Some of the industrial applications of chemistry are considered in this connection. Attention is directed also to the bearing of observed facts on chemical theories. Finally, by comparing and generalizing the result of her own experimental work, the student reaches the analytical classification, and then proceeds to apply her knowledge by working out several analyses of substances of unknown composition.

The third semester is devoted to quantitative chemistry, and the chemistry of light. In this " third course " the student pursues a laboratory study of volumetric and gravimetric methods of analysis, and an illustrated lecture and library course in spectroscopy and photography.

In the fourth semester there are two courses, one in the study of hydrocarbons and their derivatives, the other in the chemistry of water, air and food.

In the fifth semester two hours a week are given to the study of the History and Philosophy of Chemistry.

The chemical laboratories are commodious, well lighted and well ventilated rooms, containing separate tables to accommodate one hundred and four students. Each table is supplied with running water, a sink, a filter pump, gas and burners, graduated glassware,—in fact, it is intended that every table shall be supplied with every piece of apparatus, except the balance, and with all the chemicals, which are actually needed by the student who uses it. The John Guy Vassar Laboratory Fund permits all needed additions to be made. No extra charge is made for the apparatus or chemicals.

A certificate of study in Inorganic Chemistry at Vassar will be accepted in place of the corresponding course at the Woman's Medical College of the New York Infirmary.

ELECTIVE.

Course A. Description of the non-metals [4]. Second semester.

Course B. Description of the metals, Qualitative Analysis [4]. First semester. Course B presupposes Course A.

Course C. Quantitative Analysis [4]. Second semester. Course C presupposes Course B.

Course D. Organic Chemistry [2]. First semester

Course E. Sanitary Chemistry [2]. First semester. Courses D and E presuppose Course C.

Course F. General Chemistry, History and Philosophy of Chemistry [2]. Second semester. Open to Seniors only. Course F presupposes Courses A and B.

MINERALOGY.

PROFESSOR DWIGHT.

A concise course in Crystallography is given, illustrated by the best glass models of crystals, and accompanied by exercises in the determination of forms, and in goniometrical measurements. Physical and Chemical Mineralogy are then taken up partly by recitations from the text-book, and partly by oral instruction, with special reference to a proper preparation for laboratory work. In Descriptive Mineralogy, the study of the principal ores and other minerals is conducted by oral instruction based as far as possible on the actual examination of specimens distributed among the members of the class. Meanwhile, at as early a point in the course as may be praeticable, laboratory practice in the determination of minerals by the blowpipe and by chemical processes is begun and continued to the end of the semester. This work is in two courses ; the first consists of a series of prescribed experiments with known minerals, as arranged in schedules prepared by the instructor. This course is so devised, with reference to the character and range of the specimens, that by its completion the student is made quite familiar with all the more important reactions of the determinative processes.

The second part consists in the determination, by each member of the class, of a large number of selected unknown minerals.

Excursions are taken to localities of mineralogical interest.

Course A. Mineralogy, full course [4]. Dana, *Manual*, with lectures, and objective study of minerals ; laboratory practice in blowpipe determination of species. First semester.

Mineralogy, shorter course [2]. Lectures on mineral structure and composition; a brief course of laboratory exercises in the study and determination of minerals. First semester.

GEOLOGY.

PROFESSOR DWIGHT.

A brief study of Physiographic Geology is followed by a course in Lithological Geology ; the elementary principles of Petrography are here introduced ; the methods of the optical study of minerals and rocks are taught and illustrated by the use of a lithological microscope, also by class exercises in the preparation of microscopic sections in minerals with reference to their optical examinations.

Dynamical Geology is then taken up. An elementary course in Paleontology follows, illustrated by the study of specimens, and by class practice in the actual determination of species of fossils. The members of the class are also exercised in the practical cutting and mounting of large microscopic sections of fossils, and rocks containing minute fossils, by means of a specially-devised rock-cutting machine of the largest dimensions and the most perfect equipment. Historical Geology occupies the latter part of the course. Its lessons are well illustrated by a large representative set of North American fossils originally collected by the New York State Survey, also by a valuable set of European fossils.

The advanced course in this subject will consist, as the class may elect, of the study of topics in Petrology, Paleontology, Stratigraphical or Dynamical Geology. A large supply of characteristic fossils, accessible to the students, furnishes opportunities for much objective study, aided by ordinary microscopic apparatus. One of Fuess's celebrated lithological microscopes of the largest size and latest pattern affords facilities for the optical study of minerals, while the method and practice of rock-slicing are taught on a large machine of the latest improved form.

Abundant use is made of the literature in the college library, and especially of the more recent discussions of geological topics in the scientific journals, and in State and Government Reports and Bulletins.

The student is thus taught how to make research in documents carrying authority, and is also familiarized with the methods of investigating and discussing geological problems. Field-work is encouraged as far as is possible. ·

Course A. Elementary Paleontology [2]. A general course in the study of the structure and classification of plants and animals, with special reference to Geology, for which it is a very important preparation. Second semester.

Course B. Full course [4]. Dana, Text-book, with lectures. Exercises in the study of fossils and in the preparation of microscopic sections of rocks, minerals and fossils.

Shorter course [2]. Lectures on the general scope, material and methods of geological history and of dynamical geology. Second semester.

Course C. [2]. An advanced course, either in Petrography or in Paleontological and Stratigraphical Geology, with practice in field-work. First semester.

Course D. Advanced geology [2]. Either a continuation of Course C, or, for those who have not pursued Course C, a similar course. Second semester

Course C, or Course D, presupposes Course B.

BIOLOGY.

ASSOCIATE PROFESSOR O'GRADY, MISS BYRNES, MISS E. C. PALMER.

The instruction in Biology consists of lectures, recitations, and laboratory exercises.

The course in General Biology in the Junior year serves as an introduction to the study of the Biological Sciences. It is intended that this course shall give the student a clear and comprehensive conception of the fundamental principles of life.

A number of representative forms of animal and vegetable life are studied in their structure and their mode of action, to illustrate the principal facts of morphology and physiology.

This general course is followed in the Senior year by more special work in General Zoölogy and Comparative Embryology. In the first semester, the student gains a systematic knowledge of the animal kingdom, attention being paid chiefly to the classification, development and homologies of invertebrates. In the second semester Comparative Embryology is taken up. This includes a thorough study of the Embryology of the chick, followed by a comparative study of the development of vertebrates.

An additional course in higher Biology is given in the second semester of the Senior year, including some of the leading questions of Biology, such as natural selection, evolution, heredity, and the history of the Biological sciences.

The present Senior class was given in the Freshman year a required course in General Biology, and in the Junior year, a modification of the regular Senior elective, viz. General Zoölogy and Embryology. In the year '92–'93 a more advanced Senior course is offered: Vertebrate Zoölogy in the first semester, Higher Biology in the second semester, and a Biological Seminary throughout the year.

The work in Vertebrate Zoölogy is intended to familiarize the student with the more important facts relating to the structure of vertebrated animals, special stress being laid upon comparative osteology.

The object of the seminary is to gain familiarity with the methods of original research, practice in bibliography and in the presentation of papers. Each student selects a special topic which she pursues with direct reference to original research. In addition papers are presented at the weekly meetings upon current biological literature.

In the laboratory the student acquires a thorough knowledge of methods, and of the forms discussed in the lectures. An attempt is made to cultivate the spirit of original research.

Students intending to study Biology are recommended to acquire a knowledge of the elements of chemistry.

Courses A. and B.   General Biology [3]. First and second semesters.

Course C.   General Zoölogy [3]. First semester. Course C presupposes Course B.

Course D.   Comparative Embryology [2]. Second semester. Course D presupposes Course C.

Course E.   Higher Biology [1]. Second semester. Course E presupposes Course D.

*Course F.   Vertebrate Zoölogy [2]. First semester.

---

* Courses F, G, H are offered only for '92–'93.

Course G. Biological Seminary [1]. First and second semesters. Course G presupposes Course F.

Course H. Higher Biology [2]. Second semester. Course H presupposes Course F.

PHYSIOLOGY AND HYGIENE.

Dr. Thelberg.

REQUIRED.

Hygiene. A course running through the year. One hour weekly is devoted to this course, and the study comprises lectures, recitations, and practical investigation of the principles of house sanitation. Drawings and models are provided for this study. All new students are required to attend. Freshman year.

ELECTIVE.

Course A. Advanced Physiology [3]. Second semester. The course comprises lectures, text-book work, microscopic study of tissues, experiments in physiological chemistry, and frequent dissections. The Anatomical Cabinet furnishes models for practical demonstrations.

PHILOSOPHY.

President Taylor and Professor Drennan.

The study of Psychology is required of all candidates for a degree. The aim is to acquaint the student thoroughly with the principles of the science by a detailed study of the facts and processes of the mental life, and then in the study of the nature of intelligence to observe them in combination. The purpose of the instructor is to show the relation of the facts thus observed to the principles underlying the current discussions of philosophy and religion. A syllabus is used both as a guide and as a basis for discussion by the student and teacher. This course is supplemented by a course of lectures dealing with the theories of perception as they appear in the writings of modern philosophers, with the psychological and cosmological problems involved in them.

Courses of reading in the history of philosophy are assigned to the members of the class with a view to preparation for essays, or for special examination.

The course in Ethics is also required of students for a degree. The methods of instruction are similar to those outlined above. A text-book forms the basis of the work, and is made the ground of free discussion. A course of lectures supplements the work and reading in the history of ethical philosophy is required. Topics of study are the conscience, moral law, the will, and the ultimate ground of moral obligation. The relations of the principles thus discovered to the duties of moral beings to self, others, and God, are also discussed.

REQUIRED.

1. Psychology ; Lectures on Modern Philosophy [4]. Senior year, first semester. PRESIDENT TAYLOR.

2. Ethics ; Lectures on the history of Ethical Philosophy [3]. Senior year, second semester. PRESIDENT TAYLOR.

ELECTIVE.

Course A. Logic [3]. This study is offered as a three hours' course, through one semester of the Junior year. As students in Logic are often hindered in their progress by the lack of some knowledge of the nature and laws of the mind, a short outline of Psychology precedes the study of the laws of thought. Second semester. PROFESSOR DRENNAN.

History.

PROFESSOR SALMON AND ASSOCIATE PROFESSOR MILLS.

The undergraduate work in History aims to give opportunity during the Sophomore and Junior years for a somewhat comprehensive but careful study of general European history from the beginning of the mediæval period to the present time. During the Senior year facilities are offered for special work in English and American constitutional history.

The object of the instruction given is first, to emphasize the difference between reading history and studying history; second, to acquaint each student through independent work with the best methods of historical study; third, to show in the study of different nations the development of present from past conditions; fourth, to indicate the organic relation of history to other branches of knowledge.

The work of the department is conducted by means of text-books, topical outlines, lectures, and classes for special study. The students have free access to all works in the library and are trained to do independent work.

REQUIRED.

Mediæval History to Charlemagne, [3] Sophomore year, first semester. ASSOCIATE PROFESSOR MILLS.

The object of this course is to give some knowledge of methods of historical study, to review rapidly the prominent features of classical civilization, and mainly to study the history of Europe from Constantine to Charlemagne. Particular attention is paid to the development of the church and to the ascendency gained by Christianity over classical and Germanic ideals.

ELECTIVE.

Course A. Mediæval History from Charlemagne to the Renaissance [2]. Second semester. ASSOCIATE PROFESSOR MILLS.

In this, as in the preceding course, the dominating influence of the church is the chief object of attention. Feudalism, the formation of the European states, the Holy Roman Empire, the Crusades, the evidences of a new spirit as shown in the revival of commerce, city life, the revival of learning and art, are among the principal topics considered. Each student should be provided with Bryce's The Holy Roman Empire.

Course B. Modern European History [3]. First semester.
PROFESSOR SALMON.

This course comprises a special study of the political and religious condition of Europe during the fifteenth and sixteenth centuries, and the political and religious history of Europe from the beginning of the Reformation to the Treaty of Westphalia. As far as possible the period is studied from contemporaneous literature, official documents, and the leading modern authorities. It is one aim of this and the following course to give the student constant practice in the different uses of historical material, as in the preparation of bibliographies and biographies, the study of treaties and creeds from the documents themselves, reviews of recent literature treating of the period and work in historical geography.

Course C. Modern European History [3]. Second semester.
PROFESSOR SALMON.

This course is the continuation of Course B. The work comprises a brief survey of the history of Europe from the Treaty of Westphalia to the beginning of the French Revolution. A more special study is then made of the period of the Revolution and of the political development of the different countries as resulting from it. It is one object of this and of the preceding course to show by the study of comparative history the influence of different nations on each other.

Course D. English and American Constitutional History [4]. First semester. PROFESSOR SALMON.

This course is open to students who have had at least three courses in History.

The course is intended to offer opportunity for critical study of the origin and development of the English and American constitutions and a comparative study of the existing political institutions of the two countries. The specific lines of work along which the general subject is studied vary from year to year. The class is divided into small sections, thus affording opportunity for constant discussion of facts and principles and the individual study of special topics.

Course E.   American Constitutional History [3].   Second semester.
                                                    PROFESSOR SALMON.

This course is open to all Seniors.

The work comprises a study of the workings of the American constitution with special reference to the history of political parties.

Course F.   Comparative Politics [2].   Second semester.
                                                    PROFESSOR SALMON.

This course is open to those who have taken Course D.

The work comprises a study of different theories in regard to the origin and functions of the State, with an examination of the appiication of these theories in the different forms of modern federal government.   The specific questions considered vary from year to year.

ECONOMICS.

ASSOCIATE PROFESSOR MILLS.

Students intending to take but one course should elect B. Those planning to take several may begin with either A or B. The first four courses may be taken advantageously in either of the following orders : A, B, C, D ; B, A, D, C.

The methods of work in this Department will be various, depending upon the nature of the topic, the resources of the library and the object of the course. Lectures, investigation of special topics, text-books as a basis for discussion and recitation will all be used. Whenever available, Reports of National and State Bureaus of Labor, of Railroad Commissions, and of the Census Bureau and other statistical documents will be employed.

Course A.   Industrial and Economic History. [3].   (1) The development of Industrial Society ; (2) Economic and Financial History since the French Revolution.   First semester.   This course requires no previous study of Economics.

The first part of this course will deal with such topics as the following :. the English manor ; the revival of commerce and industry ; the merchant and craft guilds ; mediæval agriculture ; economic effects of the Great Plague; the growth of international trade ; the great trading companies ; progress of agriculture; domestic system of industry; the industrial revolution; the factory system. The work will be based upon the works of Ashley, Cunningham, Thorold Rogers, Toynbee, R. W. C. Taylor, Weeden. Gibbin's Industrial History of England will furnish the student an outline connecting the topics considered. The second part of the course will follow closely Rand's Economic History since 1763.

Course B. Principles of Economics [3]. Recitations from Marshall, *Elements of Economics* and Andrews, *Institutes of Economics.* Second semester.

This course is designed to give a fundamental knowledge of the main principles of economic theory with such attention to conflicting views as time permits. Collateral reading is required. Particular attention will be given to Money and Banking.

Course C. Railroad Transportation, Trusts, and the Relation of the State to Monopolies [2]. First semester. Must be preceded by B.

A study of the railroad problem gives the best introduction to a consideration of other monopolies and the attitude of the state to them. Such attention as is possible will be given to municipal monopolies. Recent legislation will be studied. This course includes a consideration of many theoretical questions that have come to the front under modern industrial conditions. Hadley, Railroad Transportation ; Dabney, Public Regulation of Railroads ; H. C. Adams, Relation of the State to Industrial Action, will be the chief books used.

Course D. The Labor Problem : its Origin and Attempts toward its Solution [2]. Second semester. Open to those having had B, and also to those having had A who take B.

The chief topics considered will be the progress and present condition of the working classes; their claims; factory legislation; history and aims of workingmen's combinations; concilation and arbitration; co-operation; profit sharing. For the present the subject of social-. ism will be included in this course.

Course E. Social Science [2]. Second semester. Open only to Seniors who have taken or who take B.

A study of some of the prominent social problems, as the family and divorce, pauperism, condition of the poor in great cities, charities, insanity, crime, modern prison science, immigration, workingmen's insurance, savings institutions.   Visits will be made to various charitable and correctional institutions, of which there is a considerable variety within easy access of the College.   The formal and informal lectures by those in charge of the institutions visited have been very instructive.

Course F.   Economic Seminary [2].   Second semester.   This Seminary will be formed only when desired by several properly prepared students.   A prerequisite for admission is the completion with success of at least three courses in Economics.   If not previously taken Course D must be elected contemporaneously with the Seminary.

ART.

Professor Van Ingen.

Four courses, all elective, are offered in this department.   One Theoretical, two Historical, one Technical.*

Course A, Theory of Architecture, Sculpture and Painting, has special reference to the principles of criticism.

Courses B and C comprise the History of Architecture, Sculpture and Painting.

Course D, Technic, lays the foundation for the work of the professional artist.

The instruction in Courses A, B and C, is given by means of lectures and collateral reading.   A large collection of Braun Photographs, Casts and Diagrams elucidates this instruction.   The work gone over in these several classes is further impressed on the student's mind towards the close of the year by a course of twelve illustrated stereopticon lectures, which bring all the prominent works of art on a large scale before them.   These lectures are open to all the members of the college.

Course A. [2].   Theory of the art of Design.   First semester.   This course comprises a study of Beauty in Art, intellectual and optical beauty.   Unity, its application to different modes of expression.   Definition of Architecture, laws derived from nature: Materials used in Architecture, their effect on construction :   Lintel and column ; round-arch and dome ; pointed arch and buttress ; the truss : Decora-

---

*For this course there is an extra charge.

tions in Architecture. . Definition of Sculpture ; the Statue ; low,
medium, and high relief ; laws of relief : Materials used in Sculpture and subjects treated. Definition of Painting; Imitation; Materials
used in painting. Etching, Engraving, Lithography, Photography.
Composition, the Sketch, the Studies. Drawing ; its importance,
Stereography, Orthography, Stenography. Perspective, the definition,
the perspective of a point. Parallel perspective, Oblique perspective, problems. The Human form in Art, Proportion, Anatomy,
Expression : Gesture, Drapery, Costume, Attributes. Chiaroscuro,
tone. Colour. Touch. Various kinds of pictures ; historical, portrait, genre, landscape, animal, battle, marine, architectural, flower,
fruit, still-life, scene and ornamental paintings.

Course B. [2]. Second semester.

History of Art, Architecture and Sculpture : The Egyptian Temple
and its Sculptures, Tombs and Sculptured Reliefs, Pre-Historic Monuments of Greece, The Greek Temple and its Sculptures, the Periods
of Phidias and Praxiteles, the Alexandrian Period, Roman Architecture, Portrait Statues and Historical Reliefs, Early Christian Architecture, the Byzantine and Latin Styles, the Romanesque and Gothic
Cathedral and their Sculpture Decorations, Renaissance Architecture
and Sculpture, Ghiberti, Donatello, Della Robbia, Michael Angelo,
Bernini, Canova, Flaxman, Thorwaldsen.

Course C. [2]. First semester.

Painting : Classic and Byzantine Painting, Renaissance Painting,
Giotto, Fra Angelico, Masaccio, Leonardo, Michael Angelo, Raphael,
Titian, Veronese, Durer, Rubens, Rembrandt, Velasquez, Murillo,
Poussin, David, Millet, Hogarth, Reynolds, Benjamin West.

Course D. Technical instruction in Drawing and Painting in Oil
and Water-Colours.

The work is graded into the following Classes :

Class 1 : Preparatory Class : Drawing in black and white and Water
Colours from Geometrical, Ornamental and Architectural forms.

Class 2 : Antique Class B : Drawing from models of parts of the
human figure.

Class 3, Antique Class A : Drawing from the full length Statue.

Class 4, Still-life Class : Painting in Oil and Water-Colours.

Class 5, Portrait Class : Drawing and Painting from the draped Life
Model.

Classes 1, 2, 3, 4, continue each through one semester ; Class 5
through two semesters, (each class two hours, three days in the week).

MUSIC.

PROFESSOR BOWMAN.

Harmony. Exercises in writing Intervals, Triads, Sept Chords, Altered Chords, Organ Point, Suspensions and Harmonic accompaniment to selected and original melodies.

Course A. Principles of Harmony [2]. First semester.

MISS BLISS AND MISS BLEWETT.

Course B. Embellished Modulations and Harmonic accompaniment [2]. Second semester.   PROFESSOR BOWMAN.

Course C. Counterpoint. Exercises in adding, one, two, three, four or more voices in Simple Counterpoint to given or original *cantus fermi.* Also the principles* employed in writing Double Counterpoint, Canon and Fugue [2]. First semester.   PROFESSOR BOWMAN.

Course D. History. It is the aim in this course to study under the following headings the outlines of musical progress from the time of the most ancient Oriental civilization to the present : Oriental and Ancient Music. The first ten centuries of Christian Music. From Guido to the Fourteenth Century. Epoch of the Netherlanders. The Rise of Dramatic Music. The Beginning of Oratorio. Instrumental Music from the Sixteenth to the Nineteenth Century. Development of Italian, French and German Opera. Development of the Oratorio, Cantata, Passion Music and Sacred Music [2]. First semester.   PROFESSOR BOWMAN.

Course E. History. This course is designed to fill in the details of the most important features in the development of music during the last hundred and fifty years. Biographic and analytic lectures are given on the chief workers and works in Opera from Gluck to Wagner, special attention being devoted to the latter. A special supplementary course is given in the History of Piano-forte Playing and Pianoforte Music [2]. Second semester.   PROFESSOR BOWMAN.

The College Chorus offers class training in the principles and practice of vocal music, such as Notation, Time, Accent, Dynamics, Tone-production, Articulation and Expression. A superior class of music is studied for practice in Interpretation and for performance at such public exercises of the College as may be thought advisable. The

---

*The Department of Music having recently been placed on a collegiate basis, some of its work is necessarily in a formative state. It is the intention to extend the time allowed for the practical study of the higher contrapuntal forms as soon as possible.

drill is divided into two parts between which, by way of interlude, the instructor gives a brief lecture on some topic pertinent to general musical culture, for example, such as : How to Study Music. Characteristics of Great Composers. Synopsis of Great Compositions. What the Musical World is Doing To-day.

PROFESSOR BOWMAN.

Instruction is also furnished by the College in the practice of music, —vocal (Mr. Sauvage), organ (Miss Blewett), piano-forte (Miss Whitney, Miss Chapin, Miss Bliss, Miss Blewett), and violin (Mr. Grube),— and for this an extra charge is made, see p. 76.

To the concerts and lectures given during the year by eminent artists and lecturers, students have free access. The College Choir offers valuable experience in church music, and the monthly meetings of the Thekla Club afford students of the piano-forte the opportunity of performance in the presence of others.

BIBLE STUDY.

The College aims to give, in a progressive course of study, such instruction as shall enable the student to gain a general knowledge of the history and teachings of the Bible. Among the specialists who have conducted this work are President Harper and Professor Burton of the University of Chicago, Professor Riggs of the Auburn Theological Seminary, and Professor True of the Rochester Theological Seminary. The course for the present semester is upon the Beginnings of the Church as seen in the Acts of the Apostles.

SUMMARY OF THE COURSES OF STUDY.

Letters indicate elective courses ; figures, the number of hours per week.

FRESHMAN YEAR.

ALL REQUIRED.

First Semester.		*Second Semester.*	
Latin	4	Latin	4
Greek ⎫		Greek ⎫	
French ⎬	4	French ⎬	4
German ⎭		German ⎭	
English	3	English	3
Mathematics	3	Mathematics	3
Hygiene	1	Hygiene	1
		Elocution	1

SOPHOMORE YEAR.

REQUIRED.

First Semester.		*Second Semester.*	
Latin	3	Latin	2
Greek		Greek	
French	3	French	2
German		German	
English	3	English	3
Mathematics	3		
History	3		

ELECTIVE.

Student to elect 8 hours.

A. Mathematics	4
A. Chemistry	4
A. Elementary Paleontology	2
A. Mediæval History	2
A. Latin	2

JUNIOR YEAR.

ALL ELECTIVE.

First Semester.		*Second Semester.*	
B. Latin	3	*C.* Latin	3
A. Greek, short course,	3	*A.* Greek, short course,	3
B. Greek	2	*C.* Greek	3
A. French, short course,	3	*A.* French, short course,	3
B. French	2		
C. French	2	*D.* French	2
A. German, short course,	3	*A.* German, short course,	3
B. German	2	*C.* German	2
A. English, Rhetoric.	2	*B.* English, Essays,	1
D. English, Shakspere,	3	*E.* English, Queen Anne,	3
F. Anglo-Saxon	3	*G.* Anglo-Saxon	2
B. Mathematics	3	*C.* Mathematics	3
A. Astronomy	1		
B. Astronomy, general,	3	*C.* Astronomy	3
A. Physics	4	*B.* Physics	3
B. Chemistry	4	*C.* Chemistry	4
A. Mineralogy	4 or 2	*B.* Geology	4 or 2
A. Biology	3	*B.* Biology	3
		A. Logic	3
B. History	3	*C.* History	3
A. Economics	3	*B.* Economics	3
A. Art	2	*B.* Art	2
A. Music	2	*B.* Music	2

SENIOR YEAR.

REQUIRED.

First Semester.		*Second Semester.*	
Psychology	4	Ethics	3

ELECTIVE.

D. Latin	3	*F.* Latin	3
A. Sanskrit	2	*B.* Sanskrit	2
D. Greek	2	*E.* Greek	3
E. French	2	*F.* French	2
D. German	2	*E.* German	2
C. Forensics	2	*I.* English Philology	1
H. Chaucer	2		
D. Mathematics	3	*E.* Mathematics	3
D. Astronomy	3	*E.* Astronomy	2
		F. Solar Physics	2
C. Physics	3	*D.* Physics	3
D. Chemistry, Organic,	2	*F.* Chemistry	2
E. Chemistry, Sanitary,	2	*D.* Geology	2
C. Geology	2	*D.* Biology	2
C. Biology	3	*E.* Biology	1
		A. Physiology	3
D. History	4	*E.* History	3
		F. Comparative Politics	2
C. Economics	2	*D.* Economics	2
C. Art	2	*E.* Social Science	2
		F. Economic Seminary	2
C. Music	2	*E.* Music	2
D. Music	2		

DEGREES.

Students who have completed the regular course will receive the First or Baccalaureate Degree in Arts (A.B.)

No person will be admitted to the College as a Candidate for the degree of Bachelor of Arts after the beginning of the first semester of the Senior year.

The Second Degree in Arts (A.M.) may be conferred upon Bachelors of Arts of this or of any other approved College, who have pursued a course of advanced non-professional study. The required period of residence is one year, but graduates of this College studying *in absentia* must employ at least two years to complete the same amount of work. Non-residents must submit to the Faculty their proposed course of study at least two years in advance. The candidates must pass examinations on the course of study arranged and present an acceptable thesis. The title of the thesis must be presented to the Faculty as early as possible and not later than January first of the year in which the degree is to be conferred. A fair copy of the thesis should be sent to the President's Office not later than May first of the same year.

The degree of Doctor of Philosophy (Ph.D.), *in course,* will be conferred on graduates of this or of any other approved College. The requirements for such a degree will be a three years' course in liberal studies, two of which shall be spent at this College, but by vote of the Faculty a year of graduate study at some other college or university may be accepted for one year of residence. Two principal subjects of study must be pursued by every candidate for the degree, examinations must be taken in both, and a thesis showing original research must be presented on one of them. The candidate must be able to read Latin, French, and German, and must have at least an elementary knowledge of Greek.

The degree in Music, Musicae Baccalaurea (Mus.B), is open to graduates of this, or of any other approved College, and to such as may produce certificates testifying to their use of at least five years in the study of Music. Two examinations must be taken by every candidate, at an interval of not less than one year, the first covering Harmony and Counterpoint in not more than four parts, and Canon and Fugue in two parts, and the second embracing Harmony and Counterpoint in five parts, Canon and Fugue, Musical Form (analysis), History of Music, and Orchestration. Before the final examination the candidate will be required to submit for the approval of the examiners a composition on a sacred or secular subject, containing some portion for a solo voice, some for a chorus for four parts using fugue treatment, and an accompaniment for piano, organ, or a string band, said composition to occupy about fifteen minutes in its performance.

Resident graduates and students in special courses, may receive from the President a certificate of the studies completed.

The degrees conferred in 1892 were as follows:

A. M.   THESES.

ANNA CLELAND MCFADDEN—A part of Caedmon's Genesis translated with vocabulary and notes.

CORA ANGELINA START—Naturalization in the English Colonies ·in America.

A. B.

ELLEN CORDELIA ABBOTT,	MARGARET MORTON,
AGNES ARBUCKLE,	EMMA LOUISE MOTT,
EDITH COLBY BANFIELD,	THEODOSIA OLDHAM,
CLARA LOUISE BARBER,	ANNA OWENS,
KATE MILLS BRADLEY,	MARY SECORD PACKARD,
REBECCA WHITLOCK BRUSH,	ANNA MATHER PALMER,
ELLA WELBON CRAMER,	ELIZABETH CUMMINGS PALMER,
EVA JOSEPHINE DANIELS,	ANNA LOUISE PERKINS,
KATHARINE BEMENT DAVIS,	ESTELLE RUTHERFORD PUTMAN,
MARY ELIZABETH FANTON,	SARA SHERWOOD PLATT,
ELIZABETH FLAHERTY,	AMY LOUISE REED,
PENELOPE MCNAUGHTON FLETT,	ALICE MARION ROBBINS,
HELEN NORTH FROST,	ELIZABETH LINCOLN ROWE,
CORNELIA GOLAY,	MILLIE BIGLOW SARGENT,
ELEANOR FRANCIS GOULD,	CARRIE MORGAN SMITH,
LAURA CHURCHILL GRANT,	MARY ALICE SMITH,
EMELYN BATTERSBY HARTRIDGE,	EDITH HELEN STEARNS,
MAUDE AMELIA HENCH,	ANNIE AGNES STEPHENSON,
PAULINE HERRING,	KATE TAYLOR,
SARAH SHEPPARD HOMANS,	KATE BARDWELL TITUS,
JENNIE ICKLER,	SARAH BACON TUNNICLIFF,
LINA BAYLIS JAMES,	ADELENE CLARKE ULRICK,

NELLIE DEAN KING,   SUSIE EMILY WAKEMAN,
HENRIETTA LOIS MANNING,   EMMA FRANCES WALLACE,
ELIZABETH MATILDA MAST,   EDITH WARD,
HELEN GULIELMA MOOREHEAD,   LUCIA EDNA WOOD,
HESTER BOTSFORD MORRILL,   SARAH ELIZABETH WOODBRIDGE.

Under the rules existing prior to this year, diplomas for the completion of the course in Painting were awarded to

MARTHA SOPHIA BENSLEY,   MARY LOUISE BURKE,
AGNES BIRKMAN,   MABEL LILLIAS COOLEY,
MABEL ELEANOR BUNTEN,   HELEN EMMA MITCHELL,
CARRIE THORNE WING.

LECTURES.

The College provides courses of lectures supplementary to its regular work. The subjects, as far as arranged, are as follows:

James Russell Lowell, ... MISS M. L. AVERY.
1. The Ancient Educational Ideals,
2. The Beginnings of the Universities,
3. The Educational Reformers,
4. The Modern State and Education,
     PROFESSOR NICHOLAS MURRAY BUTLER.
The Precursors of the Pianoforte (with illustrative music
   upon the M. Steinert collection of keyed instruments,) . .
     MR. H. E. KREHBIEL.
Early Christian Rome and the Catacombs, . MR. PERCY M. REESE.
Democracy, ... PROFESSOR WOODROW WILSON.
The South in Literature, . . . MR. JAMES LANE ALLEN.
The Early Church as seen in the Acts and the Epistles, (six-
   teen lectures), ... PROFESSOR B. O. TRUE.
1. Sociology and Social Problems,
2. Statistics, ... DR. SAMUEL W. DIKE.
The Public Schools of England, . . MR. GEORGE L. FOX.
Early Phases of Local Development as shown in the Organ-
   ization of the Native Tribes of our Country, (two lectures),
   Indian Music, ... MISS ALICE FLETCHER,
Some Aspects of the Eighteenth Century,
     PROFESSOR ALBERT TUTTLE.
Roman Life . . . . PROFESSOR JAMES B. GREENOUGH.
The Currency of the United States, . PROFESSOR F. W. TAUSSIG.
American Literature, . . . PROFESSOR BARRETT WENDELL.

Concerts are also provided for the College under the auspices of the Department of Music. They are given by artists from the best known Musical Clubs and Societies.

GRADUATE COURSES.

Courses of advanced study are offered by the various departments of the College to graduates of colleges who may prove to the Faculty their ability to profit by them. It is the purpose of the Faculty thus to encourage independent work. The student will have the advantage of study with the instructor, and of a general direction in her investigations.

Graduate courses of study, under the direction of the heads of the different departments of instruction, will be arranged for such resident graduates as wish to take examinations for the Second Degree in Arts (A. M.)

The following courses are offered for the coming year.

Ancient Languages.

Dramatic Poetry among the Romans, with special study of the early period. Latin Inscriptions.

Aristotle On the Constitution of Athens. The text will be studied from a fac-simile of the manuscript. Attic Inscriptions.

Modern Languages.

Studies in Middle High German and Old French.

Philosophy.

Locke, Berkeley, and Hume.

The History of Ethical Philosophy in England.

Natural History.

Paleontology and Geological Field-work.

Chemistry and Physics.

Any one of the following :

A course of laboratory work in Electricity.

A course of laboratory work in Light, including the spectroscope and its applications.

A course of practical Chemistry and Physics adapted to the wants of teachers.

Mathematics.

An extended course in Calculus, or Modern Analytical Geometry.

Astronomy.

Practical work in the Observatory.

English.

1. Anglo-Saxon Poetry. Beowulf finished, Andreas, Judith, Elene, Caedmon's Exodus. Sievers' grammar will be used and reference made to the various histories of Anglo-Saxon Literature.

2. Anglo-Saxon Prose. Selections from a number of prose authors. Sievers' grammar and readings in the history of Anglo-Saxon Literature as in Course I. Both of these courses imply an elementary knowledge of Anglo-Saxon,—Sweets' Reader or an equivalent.

3. Literature of the Fourteenth Century. Selections from Gower, Langland, and, if possible, other writers of the period will be read with thorough study of the grammatical and metrical forms and of the phonology. A considerable part of Chaucer will also be taken in the same manner. The course includes the history of the literature of the period both in England and on the continent.

4. Reading Courses in the later English Literature will be marked out for students who desire them, according to their stage of advancement and also their purposes and aims. This work will be supervised by the instructors, and tested by means of frequent essays, personal interviews, and examinations.

THE COLLEGE AND ITS MATERIAL EQUIPMENT.

The College is situated two miles east of Poughkeepsie, which is half way between Albany and New York, on the Hudson River Railroad. Street-cars run regularly to and from the city. The Western Union Telegraph Company has an office in the building.

The College buildings comprise the Main Building, a structure five hundred feet long, containing students' rooms, apartments for officers of the College, recitation rooms, the chapel, library, dining rooms, parlors, offices, etc.; the new Hall for residence; the Vassar Brothers' Laboratory of Physics and Chemistry; the Museum, containing the collections of Natural History, the Art Galleries, the Music Rooms, and the Mineralogical and Biological Laboratories; the Observatory; the Alumnæ Gymnasium; the Conservatory; the Lodge; Residences for Professors; and various other buildings.

The Main Building.

This building is warmed by steam, lighted with gas, and has an abundant supply of pure water. A passenger elevator is provided. Every possible provision against the danger from fire was made in the construction of the building. In addition to this there is a thoroughly equipped fire service, a steam fire engine, connections and hose on every floor, several Babcock extinguishers, and fire pumps.

The students' apartments are ordinarily in groups, with three sleeping-rooms opening into one study. There are also many single rooms and a few rooms accommodating two persons. The rooms are provided with necessary furniture, and are cared for by servants. The construction of the building is such that even more quiet is secured than in most smaller edifices. The walls separating the rooms are of brick, and the floors are deadened.

The New Residence Hall.

The College is erecting a building for the accommodation of one hundred students. It will be ready for occupancy in December. Meanwhile the numbers unprovided for in the present buildings are cared for in a hotel which has been leased by the college.

The new building is arranged in single rooms, and in suites of three rooms for two students. The dining room, the height of which extends through two stories, is at the north end of the building. Everything has been done to make this hall attractive and comfortable, and owing to the generosity of Mr. John D. Rockefeller who supplemented the appropriation by a gift of $35,000, it has been possible to provide a model building for residence.

It contains an elevator, the plumbing is of the best pattern, and it is protected against fire in the same manner as the Main Building.

The Frederick F. Thompson Library.

This building, connected with the main edifice, is now in process of construction, and it is hoped that it will be completed in the spring. Mr. Thompson's great generosity meets one of the chief needs of the college.

THE LIBRARY of the College contains about nineteen thousand volumes, selected with special reference to the needs of the various departments. Provision is made for its growth by annual appropriations. The students have free access to the shelves during eleven hours of each day.

THE READING ROOM receives, in addition to the daily and weekly papers, the leading scientific, literary, and

philological periodicals, American, English, German, and.
French.

The Vassar Brothers' Laboratory of Chemistry and Physics.

This is a large and commodious building, with rooms
of ample size for lectures, and laboratories for the practical study of general and analytical chemistry.

An addition, costing $4,000, has been made to this
structure during the past summer, and is to be devoted to
the work of experimental physics.

In the Qualitative Laboratory, two capacious ventilating
chambers divide the tables into three sections, affording
abundant facilities for the removal of noxious gases.
Every table is supplied with gas, water and waste pipe, a
filter pump, a full set of re-agents, and every utensil needed
for the work.

In the Quantitative Laboratories, each table is supplied
with Bunsen's and Fletcher's burners, water and filter
pump, a set of graduated glassware, and all the minor
pieces required for both gravimetric and volumetric analysis. Fletcher's gas furnaces for oxidation and reduc-
tion, apparatus of various forms for specific gravity, and
a full supply of chemical balances are within easy reach,
while hot water, distilled water, drying ovens, and blast
lamps are conveniently placed.

The Cabinet of Philosophical Apparatus contains a large
collection illustrating the several branches of physics.
Among the instruments of precision are the following :
Atwood's machine with electric action, a fine standard ba-
rometer given by the class of 1880, Cooley's apparatus for
precise experiments on Boyle's law, and for the electrical
registry of vibrations, tuning forks from König, a polari-
scope from Queen, a spectroscope from Hartmann and
Braun, a Mascart's electrometer, and other fine electrical
test instruments from Elliott, Breguet, Carpentier, and

Edelmann. A fund, the gift of Mr. John Guy Vassar, provides for the addition of new apparatus.

Biological Laboratory.

The biological laboratory is furnished with tables for microscopic work and dissection with re-agents, glassware and instruments, and the students are supplied with dissecting instruments, compound and dissecting microscopes, etc.

The laboratory instruments include Thoma and Minot microtomes, a Cambridge incubator, sterilizers, paraffin baths, aquaria, etc.

A valuable collection of Invertebrates from the Zoölogical Station at Naples has been added, and a series of charts illustrating the anatomy and embryology of Invertebrates.

There is a small working library in the laboratory containing the ordinary text books and works of reference and a few monographs.

The Mineralogical and Geological Laboratories.

These contain cases of representative specimens, especially intended for actual handling and study by the students of these courses. To such students they are constantly accessible. There are also various forms of requisite apparatus; among which may be mentioned a Wollaston's Reflecting Goniometer, a Joly Specific Gravity Balance, an Analytical Balance, a Fuess Lithological Microscope of the largest size and latest improved form, apparatus and re-agents for the preparation of microscopic sections of minerals and rocks, and a sufficient number of complete sets of the apparatus requisite for the blowpipe determination of minerals to furnish one to each student of the class.

A good supply of the leading text-books and books of reference on the topics studied, is furnished to the laboratories of Natural History for daily use by the students.

The Museum of Natural History.

This contains

1. The Cabinet of Minerals, Rocks, and Fossils, with more than ten thousand specimens, besides models, restorations, relief maps, sections, landscapes, etc. The minerals are over four thousand in number, all carefully selected for their educational value. There are also series of models in wood and in glass for illustrating crystallography, a series exhibiting the physical characteristics of minerals, and many duplicate specimens for manual use. The lithological collection embraces all the important rocks, about seven hundred in number ; the palæontological collection contains nearly five thousand fossils, which are chiefly from the standard European localities. There is a representative set of North American fossils, illustrating every period of geological history, and comprising over three thousand specimens, each one thoroughly authenticated.

A valuable collection of the remarkable vertebrate fossils of the Tertiary from the Bad Lands of Nebraska, including portions of gigantic mammals, also of interesting concretionary forms from the Hot Springs of South Dakota have been added.

2. The Cabinet of Zoölogy, illustrating all the sub-kingdoms, comprising about five hundred mammals, birds, and reptiles from South America ; representative vertebrates from our own country ; a collection of insects ; a choice collection of shells, corals, and other radiates ; a fine osteological series ; a set of Blaschka's life-like models of Invertebrates ; and some of Auzoux's clastic anatomical models for illustrating structural and comparative zoölogy. It is especially rich in ornithology, as it includes the Giraud collection of North American birds, well known as one of the most valuable in the United States. It contains about one thousand specimens, all mounted, representing over

seven hundred species, among which are several type specimens, and many of historical interest as the originals of Audubon's drawings. The representation of South American birds, though not so complete, is rich, embracing probably the largest series of humming birds in any College museum.

Art Gallery.

This contains a collection of oil and water-color paintings. Among these the oldest artist in America, Watson, is represented. Of the early American school it contains specimens by Trumbull, Mount, Cole, Durand, Gifford, Kensett, Edwin White, Baker. Of the later Americans it counts specimens by Inness, Boughton, Huntington, McEntee, Whittridge, Shattuck and Gignoux. Of foreign art it has works by Diaz, Courbet, L'Enfant de Metz, and Duverger. Among the water colors it counts four Turners, two Prouts, one Copley Fielding, two Stanfields and a number of others by well-known foreign and American artists.

The Hall of Casts.

Contains specimens of all the great periods of sculpture ; the Hermes by Praxiteles, the Laocoon and Niobe groups, the Sophocles and Demosthenes, the Dying Gaul and Borghese Warrior, the Venus of Milo and the Venus de Medici, the Diana, the Augustus of the Vatican, the Nuremberg Madonna, the Ghiberti Gates, the Pieta by Michael Angelo, the St. George by Donatello, a case with forty-two Tanagra figures, and a number of Architectural constructive details and ornaments. All these casts are of the size of the originals.

The art fund provides means for annual additions to the Gallery.

The Eleanor Conservatory.

This memorial gift from Mr. W. R. Farrington, of Poughkeepsie, was erected in 1886. The plants, comprising typical specimens from all parts of the world, are among the valuable resources for biological instruction. The Herbarium contains the Merrill collection of ferns and other plants.

The Anatomical Cabinet.

This contains articulated and non-articulated skeletons, a complete dissectible manikin, magnified dissectible models of the eye, ear, larynx, etc., desiccated and other specimens, comprising all that is needed to elucidate the topics studied.

The Astronomical Observatory.

The observatory contains a Meridian Circle with Collimating Telescopes, a Clock and Chronograph, an Equatorial Telescope, and two Portable Telescopes, the gifts of Dr. R. H. McDonald, of San Francisco, and Miss Cora Harrison, of the class of 1876. The object-glass of the Meridian instrument is of three and three-quarters inches diameter ; that of the Equatorial, of twelve and one-third inches. The latter is from the manufactory of Alvan Clark. A Telespectroscope made by J. A. Brashear has recently been added.

The Chapel Organ,

The gift of Mrs. John H. Deane, was constructed by H. L. Roosevelt of New York.

The Alumnæ Gymnasium.

This building, erected in 1889 by the Alumnæ and Students of the college, is the largest building for purposes of physical exercise connected with any college for women. The main part is one hundred feet long by forty-five feet wide. The upper story is used as a tennis court and as a hall for the entertainments of the Philalethean

Society. The lower story contains, besides loggia and entrance hall, a room in which there are twenty-four bath rooms, with each of which two dressing-rooms connect. At the rear of this room is a large swimming tank, the gift of Mr. Frederick F. Thompson, of New York. It is forty-three feet long by twenty-four feet wide. A well one hundred and fifty feet deep supplies it with water, which is pumped in at a temperature of from 70° to 80°.

The Gymnasium proper is sixty-seven feet long, forty-one feet wide and thirty-five feet high. It is fitted up with all the necessary apparatus, including pulley-weights, rowing-machines, quarter circles, chest developers, walking bars, swinging rings, ladders, Indian clubs, dumb-bells, and many other appliances for correcting inherited tendencies, and for developing muscle with the least expenditure of nerve force.

Health and Physical Training.

A Physician resides in the College. The health of the students is made a prime object of attention, and the sanitary regulations of the College are all carefully directed. The study of hygiene is required of all new students.

There is an infirmary with complete arrangements for the comfort of the sick, and with a competent nurse in constant attendance. It is isolated from the rest of the College, and, with a southern exposure and the cheerful appointments of its dormitories and parlor, makes a home-like place of rest for those who need temporary relief from their work.

Students who enter in good health have almost uniformly preserved it, and cases of acute disease have been very rare. Few communites of the same number of persons have so little illness.

Upon entering the College, each student is examined by the resident physician, her heart and lungs are tested, and information is solicited concerning her habits and general health. From these recorded data and measurements made by the teacher of gymnastics, exercise is prescribed to meet the special wants of each individual. This is required three times weekly unless the student is excused by the resident physician. Occasional re-examinations guide modifications of prescriptions. All exercise in the Gymnasium is under the personal supervision of the Director of the Gymnasium, who has made a special study of physical exercise as taught by Dr. Sargent of Harvard University and by other specialists. To ascertain the defeets needing correction and to avoid overtasking or wrongly working any student, the system of measurements recommended by the American Association for the Advancement of Physical Education, and adopted in all the best gymnasia, is followed. These measurements afford, as taken during several years past, interesting and encouraging information concerning the valuable effects of systematic physical education.

The Grounds of the College, covering two hundred acres, with several miles of gravel walks, tennis courts, a lake available for boating and skating, and a rink for ice skating, the gift of Trustee Rockefeller, furnish ample facilities for the out-door recreation which is required.

Religious Life.

The College is distinctly Christian; as its Founder willed it to be, and it welcomes those of every faith to its advantages. It is unsectarian in its management. Services on Sunday are conducted by clergymen of various churches, and evening prayer is held in the Chapel daily. Provision is made for the regular study of the Scriptures. Religious meetings are held Thursday and Sunday evenings. There is a Young Woman's Christian Association. Its public meetings are addressed by men and women devoted to home and foreign mission work.

The following are among the speakers from February, 1892, to February, 1893 :

Dr. Edward Judson—"New York Missions." Miss Anna L. Dawes—" The Indian Question." Dr. Samuel Dike—" Problem of the Family." The Rev. H. C. Mabie—"In Brightest Asia." Mrs. Frances J. Barnes—"Temperance in the Light of the New Testament." Dr. John G. Paton— ' Work in the New Hebrides." Bishop Hare—" Work among the Indians." Jacob A. Reis—" Children of the Poor in New York." Miss Ida Wood—"College Settlement." Mrs. Ballington Booth—"Salvation Army." Dr. Samuel Jessup— "Work in Syria " Mrs. James D. Eaton—"Work in Mexico." Miss Susan G. Chester— ' Work Among Poor Whites in the South." Signora Angelini—" Italian Protestant Missions."

Social Life.

Various societies and clubs, literary, scientific, and musical, give variety to the college life. The Philalethean Anniversary and Founder's Day furnish occasions for a more general social life.

The enforcing of the regulations agreed upon in regard to attendance at chapel, daily exercise, hour of retiring, and other matters affecting the comfort of the college life, is entrusted to a committee appointed by the Students' Association. This plan is in operation for the fourth year, and is amply justified by its results.

Expenses.

It is the aim of the College to avoid all extra charges in its proper work. Its rates are fixed with that purpose in view. The charge to all students who reside in the College is . . $400.

This includes tuition in all college studies, board, and the washing of one dozen plain pieces weekly. Extra washing is charged for at fixed rates.

·There is *no charge for board during the short vacations. No charge is made for chemicals, or for breakage in the Laboratories.*

Of the $400 there is due on entrance . . . . . $300.
And on March first . . . . 100.
Graduates of the College are received for advanced work at a
    charge of . . . . 300.
Non-resident graduates are charged for tuition in graduate
    work, ... 50.
Day students are charged . . . . 115.
Drawing and Painting. . . . . . $100 per annum.
For the Piano-forte or for Solo Singing,* two lessons
    a week, and one period for daily practice, each, 100
      Special students in music may have an ad-
ditional practice period free of charge.
For the Organ, two lessons a week. . . . 100
For the use of the Chapel Organ one period daily. 2 a month.
For the use of a piano for an additional period daily. 1 "
    For extra lessons additional charge is made at the same rates as
above.
    Students who do not take lessons may have the use of a piano for a
daily practice period at one dollar a month.

A nominal charge is made for MEDICAL ATTENDANCE.
When the student consults the physician at her office, the
charge is 25 cents ; when the physician visits the student's
room, the charge is 50 cents ; prescriptions, 25 cents each.
When a student is confined to the Infirmary, the extra
charge for regular medical attendance, medicine, and
services of nurse, and for meals served there, is $1.50 per
day. Every meal taken to a room, for whatever cause, is
charged extra.

Text-books, stationery, drawing instruments, and similar articles can be obtained at the College at current prices.

Students supply their own towels, and napkins for the
table.

Students returning after the summer vacation are not at
liberty to occupy the rooms previously assigned, until they
have made satisfactory arrangements with the Treasurer

---

*It has been found necessary to charge $150 for the singing, in order to
secure a satisfactory teacher. It is probable that it will be necessary to
continue this rate.

for the payment then due. With the exception of those about to enter College, students are not expected at the College until Friday of the opening week.

Deductions.

If the student is compelled, by sickness or other necessity, to leave the College before the end of the year for which she entered, she will be charged for board (at the rate of $8 per week) until formal notice is given by her parent or guardian that she has relinquished her room. As engagements with instructors and other provisions for the education of students are made by the College for the entire year in advance, no deduction can be made in the charge for tuition.

No deduction is made for absences during the year.

Students received at any time after the first five weeks are charged *pro rata* for the portion of the year remaining at the date of their admission. But no deduction will be made from either the regular or extra charges for the first five or the last five weeks of the year.

Scholarships.

The endowments for the assistance of students are as follows :

1. The " Auxiliary Fund " of $50,000 established by the Founder's will.

2. A fund of $50,000 established by the will of Matthew Vassar, Jr.

In awarding the latter, preference is given, to the extent of half the number receiving aid, to such as are residents of Poughkeepsie, and have been for at least five years.

The John H. Raymond scholarship of $6,000.

The Hannah W. Lyman scholarship of $6,000.

The Adaline L. Beadle scholarship of $6,000. In awarding this scholarship preference is to be given to members of the Reformed (Dutch) Church.

The A. J. Fox scholarship of $6,000, subject to the nomination of the founder.

The R. H. McDonald scholarship of $6,000, subject to the nomination of the founder.

The scholarship established by the Alumnæ of Chicago and the West. This scholarship is open to competitive examination, under the direction of a committee of the Alumnæ of that section, and it provides for the board and tuition of the successful competitor.

The Catherine Morgan Buckingham scholarship of $8,000, founded under the will of the late Stephen M. Buckingham, an honored Trustee of the College. In awarding this scholarship, it is provided that "preference shall be given to the daughters of clergymen of the Protestant Episcopal Church."

The Calvin Huntington scholarship of $6,000, established by Mr. Calvin Huntington, of Kansas. It is subject to the nomination of the founder.

The William Mitchell Aid Fund of $1,000, established by the bequest of Professor Maria Mitchell in memory of her father.

A Loan Fund from which amounts are lent to applicants, without interest.

The Merrill Fund of $10,000, the income of which "shall be applied to aid deserving daughters of foreign missionaries."

The Catharine P. Stanton Memorial Scholarship Fund of $1,000, the income of which "shall be applied for the benefit of some student in one of the higher classes of the college."

The L. Manson Buckmaster scholarship of $740.

The Matilda C. Perry scholarship of $6,000. In awarding this scholarship preference is to be given to the daughters of Baptist ministers.

The F. Helen Rawson scholarship of $6,000.

The Kittie M. Spring scholarship of $6,000.

The Charles M. Eckert scholarship of $6,000.

Applicants for assistance from any of these funds must become members of regular classes, must furnish evidence of need, and must maintain a creditable rank as students.

In addition to the above-mentioned Permanent Funds and Scholarships, there is also a College Aid Fund derived from the annual gifts of the friends of the College and of the higher education of women, as well as of persons interested in Christian education generally. This fund is usually without restriction, and from it appropriations may be made to students of any grade who may receive the approval of the Faculty.

The revenue of the College from these sources has hitherto been such that the authorities feel warranted in making the statement that students of high character and of good abilities and scholarship are seldom compelled to leave College for want of means.

As, however, the demand for aid to worthy students is constant, and as there is no probability that the demand will ever cease, the Trustees solicit the gift of more scholarships. Six thousand dollars will found a full scholarship, paying the College charges of the holder, but by a recent vote of the Trustees the number of scholarships on this basis is limited to twelve; after this number has been reached the sum of eight thousand dollars will be necessary to found a full scholarship. Partial scholarships may also be established, yielding one-quarter, one-half, or three-fourths of the income of a full scholarship; these may afterwards be completed at the convenience of the donor, and made to yield an income which shall pay all the annual College expenses of the holder.

The Trustees especially solicit contributions to the College Aid Fund, as there are often students of great promise who can be helped only in this way.

Vassar Students' Aid Society.

The Aid Society, composed of graduates, non-graduates, and teachers of Vassar College, was organized in October, 1889. The scholarships of the society are assigned as loans to applicants passing without condition the entrance examinations given at the College.

For the year '92 and '93 the General Society awarded four scholarships, two of $200 each and two of $100 each. The branches gave the following scholarships for the same year :

Boston, three of $200 each and one of $100 ; New York, one of $400 and one of $100 ; Kentucky, one of $400 and one of $100 ; Pittsburgh, one of $200 and one of $300. Tennessee gave $300 to a student already in College, and Rochester $50. Washington awarded one scholarship of $200. The California Branch gave $130 toward the establishment of the Fellowship Fund, and the Poughkeepsie Branch, not receiving applicants, turned their scholarship of $115 over to the General Society.

The following are the scholarships offered for June, 1893:

The General Society, $200. Application must be made to Miss Jessie F. Smith, South Weymouth, Mass.

The Brooklyn Branch, $200. Application should be made to Miss Jessie T. Dorman, Union Hall, Jamaica, L. I.

The Cleveland Branch, $200. Application should be made to Mrs. N. D. Chapin, 100 Kennard Street, Cleveland, Ohio.

The Illinois Branch, $200. Application should be made to Mrs. H. W. Leman, 337 Dearborn Avenue, Chicago, Ill.

The Kentucky Branch, $400. Application should be made to Miss Mary D. Anderson, Anchorage, Ky.

The Minnesota Branch, $200. Application should be made to Miss Louise B. Lindeke, 295 Summit Avenue, St. Paul, Minn.

The Orange Branch, $200. Application should be made to Mrs. James T. Dickinson, 70 East Park Street, East Orange, N. J.

The Poughkeepsie Branch, a day scholarship, $115. Application must be made to Miss E. E. Maloney, 342 Mill Street, Poughkeepsie, N. Y.

The Rochester Branch, $150. Application should be made to Mrs. W. S. Hubbell, 55 Oxford St, Rochester, N. Y.

The Tennessee Branch, $400. Application must be made to Mrs. J. L. Shotwell, 396 Poplar Street, Memphis, Tenn.

All applications must be made before April 1st, 1893.

Prizes.

By bequest of Mr. Edward M. Barringer there is a fund of three thousand dollars, the income of which is to be paid " to the best scholar in the graduating class of each year who shall be a daughter of a physician, or of one who was a physician in his lifetime, and who shall offer herself as a competitor for the prize ; " or, if no one in the graduating class presents herself, to the student in the next lower class who is eligible.

THE HELEN KATE FURNESS PRIZE FUND furnishes annually two prizes, one of thirty and one of twenty dollars, which are granted to the writers of the best two essays on some "Shaksperian or Elizabethan subject," competition being open to all members of the Senior Class. The subject is assigned a year in advance, and the essays must be presented at the opening of the second semester. The subject for the year 1893-94 will be, *Shakspere's Idea of Providence and Fate.*

The friends of the late MRS. ERMINIE A. SMITH, of Jersey City, have established a MEMORIAL PRIZE fund of one thousand dollars for excellence in the study of Mineralogy and Geology. A first and second prize will be awarded in accordance with the following extract from the deed of gift:

"The Trustees shall apply the net income from said fund as a prize or prizes to be given to any student or students of Vassar College who shall, in the judgment of said Board, from time to time have attained the highest degree of proficiency in the studies of Mineralogy and Geology."

Correspondence

The address of persons connected with the College, is *Vassar College, Poughkeepsie, N. Y.*

Letters respecting any of the departments of instruction, the admission and dismission of students, their studies, etc., should be addressed to the President. Communications in reference to rooms and the personal welfare of the students may be made to the Lady Principal.

Letters pertaining to the finances of the College, including all claims and accounts, and *requests for catalogues*, should be addressed to the Treasurer ; those relating to the general business of the College, to the Superintendent.

Teachers' Registry.

A registry of the names of students and graduates who desire to teach is kept by the College. The Alumnæ who are interested in it are requested to keep the authorities informed of changes in their residence. The President will be pleased to correspond with any who desire teachers.

Vacations and Holidays.

The College year covers thirty-eight weeks, divided into two terms, with a recess of two weeks at Christmas, and another of ten days in the spring.

Thanksgiving, Washington's Birthday, the Birthday of the Founder, and the Annual Day of Prayer for Colleges, are observed as holidays at the College. Leave of absence on these days will not be extended save for such reasons as are accepted at other times.

CALENDAR.

Anniversary of the Philalethean Society, .	December 2,	1892
Winter Holidays begin on the evening of .	December 21,	"
Winter Holidays end on the evening of .	January 4,	1893
Day of Prayer for Colleges, . . .	January 26,	"
Second Semester begins, ...	February 6,	"
Spring Vacation begins at noon on . .	March 24,	
Spring Vacation ends on the evening of .	April 4,	
Founder's Day, ...	April 28,	
Baccalaureate Sermon, ...	June 11,	
Annual Meeting of the Board of Trustees, .	June 13,	
Commencement, ...	June 14.	
Examinations for Entrance, . .	{ June 8-10, { September 20-22,	' "
College Exercises begin on the evening of,	September 22,	"
Anniversary of the Philalethean Society,	December 1,	"
Winter Holidays begin on the evening of,	December 21,	"
Winter Holidays end on the evening of .	January 4,	1894
Spring Vacation begins at noon on .	March 23,	"
Spring Vacation ends on the evening of .	April 3,	"

Lightning Source UK Ltd.
Milton Keynes UK
UKHW020623060119
334855UK00006B/423/P